MW00478071

Liberalism Defended

Liberalism Defended

The Challenge of Post-Modernity

Douglas B. Rasmussen

Professor of Philosophy, St John's University, USA

Douglas J. Den Uyl

Professor of Philosophy, Bellarmine College, USA

THE SHAFTESBURY PAPERS, 9
SERIES EDITOR: CHARLES K. ROWLEY

Edward Elgar
Cheltenham, UK • Northampton, MA, USA

© Douglas B. Rasmussen and Douglas J. Den Uyl 1997

Published by
Edward Elgar Publishing Limited
8 Lansdown Place
Cheltenham
Glos GL50 2HU
UK

Edward Elgar Publishing, Inc.
6 Market Street
Northampton
Massachusetts 01060
USA

A catalogue record for this book
is available from the British Library

Library of Congress Cataloguing in Publication Data
Rasmussen, Douglas B., 1948–
    Liberalism defended : the challenge of post-modernity / Douglas B.
Rasmussen, Douglas J. Den Uyl.
        — (The Shaftesbury papers : 9)
    Includes bibliographical references and index.
    1. Liberalism.   I. Den Uyl, Douglas, J., 1950–   .   II. Title.
III. Series.
JC574.R38   1998
320.51—dc21   97–38258
                                                                        CIP

ISBN 1 85898 557 9

Typeset by Manton Typesetters, 5–7 Eastfield Road, Louth, Lincolnshire LN11 7AJ, UK.
Printed and bound in Great Britain by Biddles Ltd, Guildford and King's Lynn

Contents

Acknowledgements

This work is in many ways a continuation of our earlier defence of liberalism, *Liberty and Nature: An Aristotelian Defense of Liberal Order* (Open Court, 1991). Further, it is part of an ongoing project. It uses and expands upon some insights from more recent defences of liberalism by us. (See our essays in Tibor R. Machan and Douglas B. Rasmussen (eds), *Liberty for the Twenty-First Century*, Rowman & Littlefield, 1995.) This work is, however, also a response to the challenge to liberalism offered by John Gray and Alasdair MacIntyre. We owe much to them for the task they have given us. Their challenge has helped us to face questions that have caused our understanding of liberalism to deepen.

Besides what is listed in the notes and bibliography, we owe special thanks to the following people for inspiration and assistance: Roger Bissell, David Gordon, Chandran Kukathas, Leonard Liggio, Loren E. Lomasky, Tibor R. Machan, Fred D. Miller, Jr and Henry B. Veatch. Special thanks are also due to an anonymous reviewer, the editors at Edward Elgar, Lucille Hartmann and, most of all, Charles K. Rowley. Finally, the following foundations and educational institutions have helped this project in various ways: Liberty Fund, The Locke Institute, Institute for Humane Studies, Bellarmine College and St John's University.

That freedom is the matrix required for the growth of moral values –
indeed not merely one value among many but the source of all values –
is almost self-evident. It is only where the individual has choice, and its
inherent responsibility, that he has occasion to affirm existing values, to
contribute to their further growth, and earn moral merit.

F.A. Hayek, *Studies In Philosophy, Politics and Economics*

1. Introduction

Why bother about liberalism? In recent times it has been pejoratively called the 'L' word. And even though the 60s generation now taking the reins of power may still see something idealistic in liberalism, the rest of us know that more government is not the answer to our problems. It may even cause many of them. The people of the United States have turned more conservative politically – especially when it comes to economic matters. Liberalism, then, seems out of step politically. That also appears to be the case intellectually. True, thinkers such as John Rawls have spawned whole intellectual industries that defend various versions of the welfare state; but one gets the sense that these efforts are more along the lines of propping up a crumbling edifice than of laying out a new direction. Why bother, then, with liberalism?

'Liberalism' in its ordinary usage is not something we would defend and, given the already existing defences, another apology would be superfluous. There is, however, one other sort of liberalism. In ordinary conversation it is often called 'conservatism', but that is a confusion. Its more precise formulation would be 'classical' liberalism. It differs from the ordinary sort of liberalism by being significantly less inclined towards programmes typical of a welfare state. We would be inclined to defend this sort of liberalism, except that within the framework of liberalism it too has been done sufficiently by others, from Adam Smith to F.A. Hayek. So, again, why bother with liberalism?

Suppose, however, that there was something that connected the two liberalisms together and which was itself under attack. Would that not indicate that a deeper and more fundamental issue was at stake? Would it not seem necessary to see what could be mustered in defence of liberalism *per se* and not just a version of it? For although we regard the ordinary or modern form of 'liberalism', as that term is used in the United States, to be a perversion of liberalism, it still holds to many of the fundamental tenets of liberalism, namely that political power is not something due anyone by natural right, that progress is possible, that the individual is the basic social unit, that people should have the freedom to pursue their own conceptions of the good life, and that the state should be limited to protecting people in the pursuit of their own conceptions of the good life. These and other principles are a part of the very nature of liberalism, and it is these very principles that are being questioned today.

Liberalism is associated with the Enlightenment which has come under serious attack in recent times. It is not just that the Enlightenment is thought to be open to some objections, but rather that it is a movement that has failed completely and has now reached its end. Liberalism is seen, therefore, as an outmoded political philosophy based upon principles that are at best naïve, but mostly just false and pernicious. Liberalism is said to undermine its own principles, to have lost any strong claims to universal validity, to subvert moral life, and to foster injustice and inhumanity. It is no longer possible, then, to defend a *type* of liberalism as if we were all agreed that liberalism is generally the correct political framework. That is no longer the case. To defend a type of liberalism, whether it be classical or modern welfare state liberalism, inevitably draws one to the deeper issues about the very foundations of liberalism. It is for these reasons that we have chosen to retain the word 'liberalism' rather than use 'classical liberalism' or 'libertarianism', even though these are the types of liberalisms closest to what we regard as defensible.

In examining the basic structure of liberalism we shall concentrate on normative issues. This makes sense because the legitimacy of the liberal order is precisely what is at issue. Moreover, people such as Alasdair MacIntyre have claimed that liberalism feeds on continual debate about its own principles to the effect that it ends up undermining its own legitimacy (MacIntyre 1988, 343–4). Liberalism must do so because it decides questions of public policy by tallying and weighing preferences about what is right or good. Yet since liberalism presents itself as being officially neutral among rival conceptions of what is right or good, the effect is to trivialize all matters of substance, since in practice all issues are reduced to preferences. Substantive moral values thereby have no more inherent worth than the most minor of policy issues. If this is a tendency in liberalism, it is certainly necessary for us to devote much of our attention to basic normative issues of how the legitimacy of liberalism is to be secured.

It may very well be that recent criticisms of liberalism have recognized a crack in which to insert a wedge. One assumption, however, goes unchallenged by defenders and critics alike: that liberalism is locked into its traditional ways of understanding itself. Liberalism has, in other words, no capacity to be linked to either pre- or post-modern thought; it is on the defensive because it is unable to incorporate anything not already found within its own Enlightenment frame of reference. It is precisely here that we believe one should bother about liberalism, for we intend to bring some 'outside' elements to bear on this debate.

Our contention is that liberalism is both defensible and capable of being enriched by other intellectual traditions. Our defence of liberalism is a defence in terms not usually associated with liberal teachings. We believe the politics of liberalism can be supported with an Aristotelian framework, at least one broadly conceived. We also argue that this framework is the *best* one for supporting liberalism. In this respect two questions are being addressed: can liberalism be supported by an alternative framework, and is that account defensible?

In addition, our discussion proceeds at a fundamental level. It is no longer enough to provide evidence that liberalism 'works' or that the alternatives to it are themselves somehow defective. Enough doubt about the justifiability of liberalism has been cast to demand some discussion of basic approaches and principles. 'Basic' here points primarily to how a moral philosophy can serve to support a political philosophy. Unlike much of liberalism, which defends its politics by resorting to either moral scepticism (the view that no one is likely to be in possession of a moral truth) or moral minimalism (the view that there are only a very few moral truths dealing exclusively with matters of social cooperation), we employ a distinction between normative and metanormative principles. The latter are most directly tied to politics and concern principles that establish the social/political conditions under which full moral conduct can take place. We do not need to minimize the moral universe to support liberalism, nor do we need to ground morality in sentiment or contracts, as much of traditional liberalism has done, to generate a liberal politics. Of course, our claim is not simply that we need not resort to traditional doctrines in defence of liberalism, but also that those doctrines create their own paradoxes, which we examine in chapter 2. Chapter 3 spells out in more detail how the metanormative approach supports liberalism, and chapter 4 responds to some contemporary critics of liberalism.

If nothing else, the crisis of liberalism is an occasion for a deepened understanding of its nature. Self-reflection usually comes at a point where what has been taken for granted has passed. Liberalism in some form has been the political philosophy of the free West for centuries. Its opponents, except the communists, were marginalized and it was taken for granted. All that has passed. The communists are now intellectually marginalized and other critics of liberalism have taken the forefront. If the period in which liberalism was unquestioned master is called 'modern', we are now in a post-modern age. To defend liberalism other than through its traditional sources must be, therefore, 'post-modern'. But if our approach is 'post-modern' it is one that does *not* succeed by rejecting the whole of modernity.

2.   Liberalism and Ethics

> He who renders to each his own through fear of the gallows is constrained
> in his action by another's command and threat of punishment, and cannot
> be called a just man. But he who renders to each his own through awareness
> of the true principle of law and its necessity, is acting steadfastly and at his
> own will, not another's, and so he is rightly termed a just man.
>
> Spinoza, *Tractatus Theologico-Politicus,* Chapter 4.

There is an ambivalence in liberalism with respect to ethics. On the one
hand, the traditional role of ethics as exhortation to appropriate conduct
seems anathema to liberalism. Leo Strauss has noticed, for example,
that:

> The soul of modern development, one may say, is a peculiar realism,
> consisting in the notion that moral principles and the appeal to moral
> principles – preaching, sermonizing – are ineffectual. And therefore that
> one has to seek a substitute for moral principles which would be more
> efficacious than ineffectual preaching (Strauss 1988, 242).

The point Strauss makes here is a feature of the broader effort by early
modern political thinkers to treat 'men as they are' rather than 'as they
ought to be.'[1] To have a social system that 'works' means that we must
discover the basic forces that operate in society and utilize this information to effectuate the outcomes we desire. The distance, therefore,
between the normative and the descriptive must not be too great, if we
are to have *workable* principles. Schemes that run contrary to basic
inclinations or rudimentary social forces will be doomed from the
outset. Ethical prescriptions, especially demanding ones, are therefore
of dubious social utility.

Indeed, as the history of liberalism unfolds, increasing attention is
devoted not to ethics but to what we would today describe as 'social
science', culminating perhaps in the science of economics.[2] From this
science (and others) it seems evident that ethical exhortations are rather
weak tools in comparison with such forces as monetary incentives
when it comes to controlling behaviour on either an individual or social

level. It is perhaps no accident, then, that the fathers of liberalism were also the fathers of economics.

We can, however, look now to the other side. Freedom of thought and speech, along with toleration, were central features of the doctrines of early liberals. Moreover, peace, social order, material well-being and the benefits that flow from any realization of these values (the alleviation of poverty, ignorance and disease) were certainly also a part of the value structure of early liberalism. In addition, the language of liberalism was, and still is, framed in terms of rights – hardly a concept devoid of moral connotations. It could be argued, consequently, that as interested as liberals were in social science, they were equally as adamant about the moral justification and propriety of the liberal order.

Nevertheless, in liberal theory the descriptive and prescriptive (social science and normative ethics) seem to have a peculiar relation to one another. It is never clear which one is to dominate, yet neither seems able to survive on its own and still function as part of liberalism. The descriptive needs the prescriptive to support the notion that the conclusions of social science should have a bearing on public policy. The prescriptive needs the descriptive to present itself as realistic and to indicate the limiting characteristics of traditional social orders. For it is clear that traditional (that is, non-liberal) orders command a certain conformity of conduct that must inevitably place limitations on someone's free pursuit of his own ends. This limitation goes beyond what is a necessary consequence of the mere adoption of any rules whatsoever; for the limitations imposed by non-liberal orders are the sort that demand an orientation of individual purposes in light of a particular conception of the good.

It might be said, then, that liberalism seems to differentiate itself from other social orders by not trying to direct individuals towards some particular and socially uniform conception of the good. Thus it would seem to have less need of moral exhortation, and only then *in addition* to the other more 'effective' techniques discovered by social science. By the same token, however, liberal orders want to be considered as having at least equal moral standing to that of any other regime, but how far can it do this in the absence of traditional exhortation or a conception of the good?

While liberalism may have a certain ambivalence towards traditional moral exhortation, its critics have none when it comes to exploiting that ambivalence to their advantage. On the one hand, liberals are criticized for not adhering closely enough to the descriptive side of their theory in their positing of universal rights independent of all social contexts. It is argued that such moral claims ignore the very reality of moral prescriptions which necessarily occur in specific social orders and practices (compare, for example, MacIntyre 1981, 65). On the other hand, liberals are accused of abandoning the prescriptive side by a narrow *homo economicus* or 'atomistic' conception of human beings which serves to undermine the very possibility of moral values.

That these criticisms have hit their mark seems to us indicated by the recent attempts by defenders of liberalism to characterize liberalism as plausible because disagreements over the nature of the good are essentially intractable (Guttman 1985). If the good is intractable, it is not clear what it would mean to claim that liberal regimes can, after all, be defended on ethical grounds. One can beg all the important questions by suggesting that intractable disagreements about 'the good' say nothing about disagreements concerning 'the right'. To make this sort of response is ultimately question-begging, because it presupposes a distinction that opponents of liberalism may say is at the heart of what they are rejecting. It seems worthwhile, therefore, to give this sort of distinction further examination.

THE GOOD AND THE RIGHT

In an effort to accommodate both personal freedom and the demands of justice, liberalism would appear to require a basic distinction such as the distinction between the good and the right.[3] The general tendency has been to consider the good as essentially privatized and the right universalized. The good, in other words, comes to be regarded as the object of one's own interest and stands in contrast to what one may do with any right. What one may do by right is what is allowed to, or demanded of, all agents (or derived from such). Early liberal thinkers could speak comfortably of the 'rights of man', but it would be unusual for them to speak of the 'good of man'. The 'goods of men', by contrast, would have been an acceptable locution (just as 'the right of man' would not). These locutions suggest that the good and the right need not have any necessary connection to one another. What one may do or possess by right has no necessary connection to what will advance one's good; and what will advance one's good may conflict with conduct allowed or demanded by right. This asynchronous character of the good and the right is due in the end to the good being partial, interested and hence amoral, while the right captures the moral by being disinterested or impartial.

Nevertheless, the distinction between the good and the right in no way diminishes the fact that one of the central problems of liberalism has traditionally been otherwise to align or harmonize the two.[4] Indeed the very nature of the distinction creates a tension in search of a resolution, and a number of resolutions have been tried. For example, social contract theory, whether classical or contemporary, could be said to be the endeavour to generate the right from the good. Those rules that shall govern the social order (the right) are to be the product of the interaction of individuals pursuing their own interests (the good). If it all works out, the governing rules are the ones we recognize to be in our own interest (for our own good).

This process may indeed reconcile the good and the right, but one is left wondering whether our satisfaction with the various descriptions of the good is simply a function of what we have predetermined to be right. In other words, are not the constraints placed upon the contractors (whether they be 'veils of ignorance' or 'unanimity') a reflection of some conception of the right, and is it not that conception of the right that tells us what is most significant about the version of liberalism being advanced?[5]

As a consequence of the nagging suspicion that social contract theories are, after all, driven more by the right than the good, some have argued (probably beginning with Kant) that the foundations of liberalism must be deontic – that is, grounded in an appeal to principle, rather than consequences (see Mack 1995). In most cases, the good (interest) is simply rejected as being relevant to any determination of the right. The irrelevance of the good can take one of two forms: either the good is irrelevant because it is beneath the right or it is irrelevant because it is above it.

In the first case, the good is defined in terms of interest and then taken to be irrelevant to the determination of one's basic duties or obligations. Instead certain generic features of personhood, for example, might serve as the basis for generating primary rights or obligations.

In the other case, the good becomes heroic because it is pitched beyond what duty requires. For example, it may be that one deserves moral credit for giving aid to another while at the same time being under no obligation to do so. The other person has no right, let's say, to the one's resources. But it seems odd to suppose that the act of charity in question has no moral value whatsoever. Consequently, the good gets recognized as a moral one but then relegated to the category of the heroic. It has little or nothing to do with the determination of the right.[6]

There is a remaining possibility under the deontic rubric. This is the situation where one's good gets defined as being *equivalent* to actions performed from a recognition of the right. Here we are usually confronted with a 'true' good – that is, one that may conflict directly with our personal interests but that nevertheless embodies a certain principle or serves a larger universal purpose. A person might, for example, be told that his personal utility ought to match the utility of society as a whole, or that his own true good consists in respecting the rights of others.[7]

In this deontic context, the 'true' good does not simply mark the classical (that is, pre-modern) distinction between the apparent and real good. The classical view still held to the notion that the 'real' good was a good for particular persons. The modern deontic view, by contrast, holds the true good to be applicable to no one in particular and everyone equally. The true good is true precisely because it purges all elements of particularity, and thus it is only *one's* good to the extent one is undifferentiated.

One final possibility of reconciling the good and the right seems to be reflected in the theories of some 18th century liberals, where the good and the right, though distinguished, were nevertheless in a kind of natural harmony or equilibrium. If, for example, people would only adhere to rights respecting conduct (for example, act without recourse to force or fraud), the diverse pursuit of their own particular good would eventually redound to everyone's benefit. This sort of Smithian invisible hand concept is, we believe, more powerful than it has been given credit for,[8] but it does little to solve the priority problems we have been addressing. For if the invisible hand does not so steadily lead to harmony, the priority question again emerges. Moreover, the very idea of harmony presupposes the possibility of separation and disharmony, so one cannot assume away the priority question.

Our brief survey suggests that there is an inevitable tendency in the distinction between the good and the right to depreciate the moral nature of the good to the enhancement of the right. In other words, what is impartial and universal comes to take precedence over goods which are, almost by definition now, partial and particular.[9] The problem, then, of separating the good from the right[10] is that particularized ethical content is increasingly sacrificed to abstract and universalized norms. Consequently the individual, thought to be so central to liberalism, becomes ethically ever more irrelevant.

If liberalism eschews moral exhortation as a technique of social management, it is not simply due to its ineffectiveness. In spite of any rhetoric to the contrary by critics and defenders alike, *liberalism is not traditionally an individualistic ethical theory*. Quite the contrary; it gives the individual good, little or no moral standing. And while liberalism may speak of individual autonomy or personhood, its universalistic tendencies render any substantive individualism almost meaningless. This is because, as we have been noting, the distinction between the good and right inevitably raises a priority question which, under the universalistic tendencies of liberalism, gets resolved in favour of the right. Individual autonomy would, for example, be good because it has initial permission to be such by the right, not right because it contributes to the good (*pace* Mill).[11]

It shall be our contention that liberalism is quite correct to ignore the individual and be universalistic in its outlook. It is, however, correct in doing so only if it relinquishes all pretences to being an ethics.[12] Liberalism is no more an ethics than it is a theology. Yet while liberalism has managed to shed any connections to theology, it has failed to distinguish itself from ethics. Liberal theorists have retained the idea that politics is ethics writ large and that therefore liberal political principles are straightforward ethical principles like any others.

For liberalism the cost of retaining this way of looking at things has been the separation of the right from the good, because it is difficult for ethical principles to be both universal and particular if there is any real diversity at the particular level. To avoid the inconveniences a diversity of particulars would pose for ethical principles, there is an inevitable tendency to generalize or universalize, that is, to count as ethical only that which can be asserted equally across persons. This, however, has the effect of undermining the moral propriety of the individualism that liberalism is supposed to cherish and foster.

The endeavour to maintain the idea that political principles are ordinary ethical prescriptions broadly extended actually has the effect of socializing ethics, that is, of giving the individual little or no ethical significance. This is exactly what one finds in the depths of liberal theory. By removing the ethical significance of individual pursuits the socialization of ethics played an important role in establishing the eventual priority of the right over the good. As a consequence, ethical norms in a liberal environment became increasingly identified with justice. Classical liberalism, in its effort to maintain the value of individual liberty, drifted inevitably towards a moral minimalism, since that best justified diversity.[13] The so-called 'new liberalism'[14] thought that moral minimalism permitted all sorts of social abuses and sought to give justice a more expanded conception, since as liberals they too were compelled to hold that the only legitimate function of the state was the enforcement of the rules of justice. Our focus below, however, will be on indicating the ways in which liberalism has socialized ethics and not upon the divergent implications of that phenomenon.

THE SOCIALIZATION OF ETHICS

Within the very seeds of liberalism[15] we find the phenomenon to which we have just referred. Consider the following from Thomas Hobbes:

> [T]hat moral virtue, that we can measure by civil laws, which is different in different states, is justice and equity; that moral virtue which we measure purely by the natural laws is only charity. Furthermore, all moral virtue is contained in these two. However, the other three virtues (except for justice) that are called cardinal – *courage*, *prudence*, and *temperance* – are not virtues of citizens as citizens, but as men, for these virtues are useful not so much to the state as they are to those individual men who have them. ... For just as every citizen hath his own private good, so hath the state its own public good. Nor, in truth, should one demand that the courage and prudence of the private man, if useful only to himself, be praised or held as a virtue by states or by any other men whatsoever to whom these same are not useful. So, condensing this whole teaching on manners and dispositions into the fewest words, I say that good dispositions are those which are suitable for entering into civil society; and good manners (that is, moral virtues) are those whereby what was entered upon can be best preserved. For all the virtues are contained in justice and charity (*De Homine* XIII, 9).

Notice how all the virtues are reduced to two, and the two virtues are themselves virtues because of what they contribute to social cooperation. The passage begins with Hobbes correctly identifying that the cardinal virtues, with the possible exception of justice, were historically centred around the perfection of the individual (one's 'private good'). And although he seems to allow for the distinction between the private and public good, the reduction of all virtues to two, and the interpretation of those two virtues exclusively in terms of their contribution to social cooperation, renders the good of individuals otiose as an ethical category. The 'private good' thus disappears as being of ethical significance, however important it may be in describing life in the state of nature or predicting the terms of the social contract.

Other liberals, or figures important to its development, make similar suggestions. Consider the following from Lord Shaftesbury:

> We may consider first, That PARTIAL AFFECTION, or social Love in part, without regard to a compleat Society or Whole, is in it-self an Inconsistency, and implies an absolute Contradiction. Whatever Affection we have towards any thing besides our-selves; if it be not of the natural sort towards the System, or Kind; it must be, of all other Affections, the most dissociable, and destructive of the Enjoyments of Society: If it be really of the natural sort, and apply'd only to some one Part of Society, or of a Species, but not to the Species or Society it-self; there can be no more account given of it, than of the most odd, capricious, or humoursom Passion which may arise. The Person, therefore, who is conscious of this Affection, can be conscious of no Merit or Worth on the account of it (Shaftesbury cited in Selby-Bigge 1897, 1:40).

David Hume makes a similar comment: 'But on the whole, it seems to me, that, though it is always allowed, that there are virtues of many different kinds, yet, when a man is called virtuous, or is denominated a man of virtue, we chiefly regard his social qualities, which are, indeed, the most valuable' (Hume, *Enquiry Concerning the Principles of Morals*, Appendix IV). Such remarks are not limited to British Empiricists. Kant claims, for example, that, 'we have reason to have but a low opinion of ourselves as individuals, but as representatives of mankind we ought to hold ourselves in high esteem' (Kant 1930, 126).

It might be objected, especially with authors such as Hume, Smith and Kant, that they were careful to separate the self-regarding from the social virtues or duties, both of which are necessary for a complete account of morality. This objection, however, simply reinforces the point. Whatever independence the self-regarding virtues or duties may possess, their value is determined almost completely in terms of their contribution to social cooperation. Consider, for example, these words from Smith:

> That wisdom which contrived the system of human affections, as well as that of every other part of nature, seems to have judged that the interest of the great society of mankind would be best promoted by directing the principal attention of each individual.to that particular portion of it, which was most within the sphere both of his abilities and of his understanding (Smith, *The Theory of Moral Sentiments*, VI.ii.2.4).

Thus although liberalism may grant the individual freedom to act as he or she pleases, this in no way implies an *ethical* individualism. And while critics of liberalism[16] are eager to point to the 'atomistic' or 'possessive' character of individuals found within liberal theories, the fact is that liberal theory is historically driven by the need to socialize rather than atomize. It is little wonder, then, that by the time one gets to Smith and Kant impartiality is the central feature of ethical theorizing, the partiality of individuals being considered the main obstacle to social cooperation and peace. It is also, in this connection, quite telling that the attack on liberalism begins in earnest with one who actually does attach positive normative value to the truly atomized individual, namely Rousseau and his 'savage man'.

That ethics is socialized under liberal theory, and therefore that traditional liberal theory is not an ethics of individualism, is itself a function of the abandonment of another feature of classical ethics – the replacement of prudence by justice as the supreme cardinal virtue. That justice could come to replace prudence is undoubtedly at least partially due to the abandonment of 'self-perfection' in favour of social cooperation, harmony or peace. Apart from what is indicated in the Hobbes passage already cited, there is little doubt that other thinkers are equally insistent upon making the substitution. Consider, for example, these passages from Hume and Mill, respectively:

> The necessity of justice to the support of society is the SOLE foundation of that virtue; and since no moral excellence is more highly esteemed, we may conclude, that this circumstance of usefulness has, in general, the strongest energy, and most entire command over our sentiments. It must, therefore, be the source of a considerable part of the merit ascribed to humanity, benevolence, friendship, public spirit, and other social virtues of that stamp; as it is the SOLE source of the moral approbation paid to fidelity, justice, veracity, integrity, and those other estimable and useful qualities and principles (Hume, *Enquiry Concerning the Principles of Morals*, Sec. 3, Pt. 2).

> It appears from what has been said, that justice is a name for certain moral requirements, which, regarded collectively, stand higher in the scale of social utility, and are therefore of more paramount obligation, than any others. (Mill, *Utilitarianism*, Ch. 5, Paragraph 37).

The urge to equate justice with the whole of ethics is virtually irresistible to liberalism. From one perspective, if liberals take the proper province of state action to be limited only to matters of justice, then all matters of serious moral concern become relegated to issues of justice. For to leave a serious moral matter outside the sphere of justice would deprive it of sanction and render it a mere matter of individual choice. It is not clear, in such a case, how serious the moral matter could therefore be if, being now left up to the individual alone, it fails to be *necessarily* social in nature and without social sanction.

Looked at from another perspective, the socialization of ethics would indicate that what is necessarily and inherently social would come to have primacy of place over that which is not. Justice would seem to be the best candidate for being central to ethics because of its apparently inherent interpersonal structure. In addition, the interpersonal character of justice seems to legitimize the *management* of interpersonal relations, bringing us back again to politics.

Since the socialization of ethics through justice tends to focus ethics upon what *can* be managed, one effect of this is to secularize ethics. Personal salvation, for example, which might have historically made some claim to primacy, is pushed to the fringes of private conscience. If social cooperation is our end, our actions or dispositions towards others must be paramount. That leaves little room for the personal or 'private' to have much standing, and it provides an incentive to interpret whatever may have been private in a public way. It is no accident, therefore, that despite Hobbes's distinction between justice and charity, the latter concept has little independent value. Spinoza is even more explicit in this connection (Spinoza, *Tractatus Theologico Politicus*, Ch. XIV). Today, of course, we have virtually no conception of charity beyond what one does for others.[17]

A further indication of the reduction of ethics to justice comes with respect to the language of rights. Communitarians often lament the fact that ethics is conducted almost exclusively in the language of rights. At least as a descriptive matter, the communitarians are surely correct in identifying rights as the central concept of liberal ethics. Indeed, among contemporary political philosophers the problem of political philosophy seems to be exclusively one of justifying and specifying basic rights. It almost goes without saying that such concerns fall under the rubric of justice. And although the various theories and their conclusions differ with respect to what rights we do or do not have, they seldom deviate from the path of seeing ethics primarily in terms of issues of justice.

For the liberal, however, a certain significant problem arises when ethics is socialized through justice. The doctrine is called 'liberalism' because of its liberal character – that is, its love of liberty. But the combination of liberty with the socialization of ethics would tend towards moral minimization. If, in other words, one's central moral obligations tend to be defined in terms of what one owes others, and one should also be left free to pursue one's own interests as one sees fit to the maximum degree possible, then squaring these two would seem to require a minimal amount of restrictive interpersonal duty.

True, one might claim that while our interpersonal duties are kept to a minimum, we may have many other moral obligations we would need to attend to as individuals. These other obligations would suggest that moral minimalism is not necessarily accurate as a description of liberalism. But as we have seen all along, what does not enter the central fold is spun off to the edges and rendered insignificant. As a consequence, liberalism seems torn between maximizing liberty and minimizing obligation on the one hand, or increasing obligation at the expense of liberty on the other. This tension is created precisely because liberty itself gets filtered through justice.

If cooperation is possible with minimal constraints upon one's conduct, then it would seem that the demand of justice has been met. If, on the other hand, the sort of 'cooperation' that results from free association is considered to be in some way defective (for example, paying workers 'starvation' wages), then the push for the inclusion of other values besides liberty will inevitably restrict liberty. The tension seems to us irreconcilable so long as justice defines the structure of ethics and liberalism is itself regarded as an ethics.

For why and whether we should value liberty more or less than something else is a question whose answer will give content to the very meaning of social cooperation and thus to justice itself; that in turn can only be resolved either by an appeal to something beyond what is in dispute, namely beyond the meaning of social cooperation (and thus beyond liberalism), or by a practical solution which decides the meaning in terms of present sentiments or customs (but leaves the issue unresolved intellectually).

THE METANORMATIVE SOLUTION

We have seen that the relationship between liberalism and ethics is one of ambivalence and tension. This ambivalence and tension results from the failure of liberal thinkers to appreciate the true uniqueness of liberalism. These thinkers write as if they were simply continuing a long tradition in political philosophy of searching for the best social order, the good society or the ideal state. They regard their project as one of producing and justifying regulative norms for the best society which have the status of moral duties.

One recent author, for example, tells us that liberalism is a, 'normative political philosophy, a set of moral arguments about the justification of political action and institutions' (Kymlicka 1989, 9). From this description one could presume that there are moralities for personal conduct, membership of a club, and relations with one's spouse, business partner or friends, as well as for 'political action and institutions'. What exactly makes all these things 'moralities' is not made explicit, but apparently they are differentiated by their subject alone.

Another writer tells us that there is an 'opposition...between liberal individualism in some version or other and the Aristotelian tradition in some version or other (MacIntyre 1981, 241), as if liberalism were a philosophy of ethical individualism to be contrasted with other ethical philosophies.[18]

Herein lies much of the problem. Norms are not, in fact, all of one type, differentiated by subject or thinker alone. It may be that some norms regulate the conditions under which moral conduct may take place, while others are more directly prescriptive of moral conduct itself. In light of this possibility, we believe it is not appropriate to say that liberalism is a 'normative political philosophy' in the usual sense. It is, rather, a political philosophy of metanorms. *It seeks not to guide individual conduct in moral activity, but rather to regulate conduct so that conditions might be obtained where moral action can take place.* To contrast liberalism directly with alternative ethical systems or values is, therefore, something of a category mistake.

Liberalism is best understood if it is not treated as an equinormative system.[19] Equinormative systems are those which regard normative principles as differing only with respect to subject matter and not type. Another way of putting the matter is to say that in equinormative systems all justified norms regulative of the conduct of persons have status as moral rules. Some rules may be more important or more fundamental than others, more or less general, or more or less about one subject or another, but they all form a single class of moral rules differing only with respect to their degree of obligatoriness or point of applicability.

Political theory is seen, then, as an extension of a debate about the merits of various equinormative systems, for example, where one system requires that individuals are to be given basic abstract rights versus another where their duties are defined by a community to which they are subservient. Theorists invest their time in working out the implications of the various systems as well as how one might be superior to another. Common to all the approaches, however, is the idea that the end product is understanding what sort of moral orientation or outlook, whether it be 'liberal' or not, communities ought to have.

It is important to understand that the position we take against the usual views about liberalism – namely that it should be viewed in terms of metanorms rather than norms – is not another version of the priority of the right over the good. One is not necessarily outside an equinormative system when deontological principles trump 'teleological' (consequentialist) ones. All that may be established is the priority of the principles, not their kind. The same point would apply to systems (for example, utilitarianism) which give priority to the good over the right, for this too may be another priority matter. Indeed modern deontological and utilitarian ethical systems, being universalistic and inclusive in nature, have little sense of a typology of normative principles, although we are not claiming they necessarily preclude that typology.[20]

It is especially important, in addition, to note that theories sceptical of systematic ethics, such as one might find in Gray or Berlin, are also equinormative. To say that there are irreducible conflicts of value does nothing to suggest that the values or norms in conflict are of a different type. Indeed in some respects this sort of theory is the most equinormative of all, since conflicts are more apparent when values or norms hold the same status.

Our view, therefore, is simply that the malaise of liberalism is largely the result of treating it as an equinormative system. Liberalism is both more vulnerable to its critics and subject to its own 'tensions' when understood in this way. The point here is not merely of a theoretical nature, but of a practical one as well. It is quite possible, as some critics of liberalism have claimed, that the exclusive focus upon liberal values has led people to ignore other significant moral virtues and has thereby impoverished morality in the process.

If, however, liberalism is not an ethical philosophy, the promotion of 'liberal values' would hardly qualify as completing a process of ethical instruction and could not be faulted as such. Nor could one claim much by way of ethical accomplishment when one succeeds in *living* according to liberal values.[21] The traditional litany of liberal values says next to nothing about what it would take for an individual to exhibit moral excellence – a point critics of liberalism are quick to make (see, for example, MacIntyre 1981, Chapters 17 and 18). There is nothing particularly laudable, challenging or directive, in other words, about being, for example, a tolerant or an autonomous individual. That would depend in large part on what one is tolerant of or that with respect to which one is autonomous.

It is nonetheless tempting in this connection to see liberal principles as implying moral values. Charles Taylor, for example, tells us that:

> To talk of universal, natural, or human rights is to connect respect for human life and integrity with the notion of autonomy. It is to conceive people as active cooperators in establishing and ensuring the respect which is due them. And this expresses a central feature of the modern Western moral outlook (Taylor 1989, 12).

If liberal principles are metanorms, it is not at all permissible, contrary to Taylor, to derive or infer moral norms or values from them, however comfortable the fit may appear. Whether individuals actively cooperate in ensuring the respect that is due to them or passively languish in the hope of that respect is of no official interest to liberalism. Because liberalism is not an equinormative system, no particular set of moral values is dictated by it, although some values may be ruled out and various ranges and sets of values may be more workable than others, depending on circumstance. It is not, in other words, any more an implication of liberalism that one's life be justified according to the dictates of the Protestant work ethic than it is by working for causes in support of gay rights. Liberalism, then, is not designed either to promote, preserve or imply one form of flourishing over another. It is not thereby completely open-ended, however. Liberalism does prevent forms of flourishing which inherently preclude the possibility of the taking place alongside of other diverse forms of flourishing.

In this respect, it may be impossible for any equinormative system which must of necessity treat its norms, however abstract and general they may be, as implying a certain form of life finally to embrace diverse forms of flourishing.[22] This is why it seems more preferable to allow ethical norms to be substantive under the umbrella of metanorms, rather than increasingly to universalize and abstract the norms themselves.

When one does treat liberalism as an equinormative ethical theory one misses an important element of liberalism, that is, its claim about the ill-suitedness or inappropriateness of the state to regulate or promote moral conduct. It makes no difference whether the conduct accords with liberal or conservative, ancient or modern, commercial or pastoral values. Liberalism's true uniqueness as a social doctrine is its endeavour to distinguish ethics from politics in the same way everyone has recognized is the case with respect to theology.

When politics is used to promote particular ethical norms or modes of flourishing, the same mistake would be committed as if it were trying to instil a particular way of understanding God or religion. Liberalism is designed to transcend[23] the competition between equinormative frameworks. The metanormative solution thus calls a halt to the discussion of whether liberalism is an adequate ethical philosophy, by suggesting not only that it is not an ethical philosophy *per se*, but also that it is in the nature of politics to imply one form of flourishing over another, when politics is used as a vehicle for the regulation of ethical conduct. What liberalism presents instead is a doctrine that separates politics from ethics as far as possible without lapsing into either relativism, nihilism or historicism.[24]

In actual practice the debate about these matters today contains a mixture of the normative and metanormative; but the failure to sort out the levels of argument – or even to recognize that there are such levels – is virtually equivalent to denying them. The Taylor passage cited above, for example, clearly indicates how normative levels are simultaneously jumped. The formalistic and abstract requirement to give persons respect in order to establish human rights is structurally different from the respect one may claim because one wishes to secure one's autonomy or be appreciated for one's worth as a person, yet they are treated the same. In the former case (human rights), any norm exists independently of who or what one is in particular, one's narrative history, one's projects, and one's links to the narratives and projects of others. The other sort of norm would be critically dependent on such factors.

The classical (that is, Aristotelian) moral perspective we adopt makes it easy for us to distinguish the morally normative from the metanormative. From the classical perspective, moral conduct, and thus the norms that regulate and define it, has as its object the self-perfection of the individual. The line of demarcation between the normative and metanormative is thus relatively easy to draw, because norms not directly concerned with the self-perfection of particular acting agents would not be 'moral' in our sense of the term.

Therefore, to advance the notion that conditions of equal freedom should obtain among individuals in society might be an important normative social principle, but in itself it does little directly to further the self-perfection of any individual. It is therefore not a moral norm but a metanorm. In this respect it is important to realize that it is not the abstractness or generality that determine metanormativity. Nothing could be more abstract and general than 'do good and avoid evil', but this principle is clearly and directly regulative of personal conduct and is thus an ethical norm.

To some, however, all this may look like begging the question. After all, why should others look at morality this way, especially since morality is more commonly viewed otherwise? We do not think the metanormative distinction *requires* adopting our approach to ethics, although we shall argue further for its appropriateness in what follows. All that is required for the plausibility of the metanormative distinction is the possibility of recognizing a difference between norms which directly regulate moral conduct and those which regulate the conditions under which such conduct could take place.[25]

Two objections come immediately to mind from what we have said: (1) that there is no material difference between liberalism seen as a metanormative system and liberalism seen as a substantive ethical philosophy, because the metanorms will in fact engender the sorts of moral values liberals have traditionally admired; and (2) liberalism would appear to be committed to a strict neutrality due to its apparent amoralist transcendental commitments; and, if not, its deepest theoretical commitments would show after all that it is an equinormative theory like any other, as suggested by the first objection.

Taking the second objection first, the exact connection between liberalism and ethics must await the following sections. The purpose here must be first to remind ourselves that liberalism is not all-inclusive, and second that to say that 'liberalism is neutral' usually means that the right takes priority over the good and liberalism is neutral with respect to forms of the good. While it is mistaken to speak of liberalism as neutral in this sense, if one must talk this way, metanormativity would imply that liberalism is as 'neutral' with respect to the right as it is to the good. We believe, however, that the right and the good cannot be separated and that liberalism is quite compatible with a perspective which denies that separation.[26] It would therefore seem necessary to focus on the first objection.

To answer the first objection fully would take us far beyond what can be accomplished here. Part of our answer occurs in the sections which follow, particularly the one dealing with the conservative communitarian alternative. It must at the same time be recognized that part of the answer also lies in one's view of the relationship between theory and practice. If a traditional society, for example, were to liberalize and allow its members the liberty to pursue their own projects, which turned out to be primarily commercial in nature, would we say the commercial ethic is an implication of the newly adopted doctrine of liberalism, or that commercial pursuits are a natural human endeavour now given the freedom to be exercised?

Ever since Plato and Aristotle it has been believed that the constitutional structure of a regime at least influences, if not creates, the sort of persons one finds in the regime. Liberal regimes would, therefore, create a certain type of 'liberal' personality, while other regimes would do likewise (see, for example, Lerner (1979)). There is undoubtedly truth in this position, though less than would satisfy the vanity of political theorists and philosophers who seem to judge their every notion as fraught with clearly delineated real world applicability.

It is quite possible, by contrast, that the structure of a regime is a function of the people within it. Liberalism does not so much answer the priority question as it does point to an alternative conception. What liberalism implies, being grounded in metanorms rather than moral duties, is that the actual social and cultural implications of its principles remain to be worked out, indeed cannot be developed except in practice.

In this sense liberalism is radically incomplete. If there is such a thing as a 'liberal' personality, it is a severely underdetermined creature. While some would suggest that it is this very underdetermination that subverts the substantive components needed for both communal and personal flourishing, liberalism's retort is that flourishing is not in the end completely written into the structural principles of any regime.[27]

Liberalism's fundamental metanormative structure indicates that ethical conduct and ethical flourishing are to be found elsewhere from politics. The apparent *laissez-faire* posture towards ethics is not a sign of rejection but of recognition that ethics is grounded in practices that cannot be subsumed by the state, or law, or even the formally constituted community. The metanormative structure is simply the recognition of that fact.

We are still left, however, with the question of how we do see the role and nature of ethics in light of this metanormative framework. To deal effectively with that question, we must first understand something of the nature of the approach to ethics we adopt and then how that approach lends itself to a metanormative understanding of liberalism.

3. The Foundations of Liberalism

For if our virtues did not go forth of us, 'twere all alike
As if we had them not

Shakespeare, *Measure for Measure*

NEO-ARISTOTELIAN ETHICS

There is available to liberalism an ethical view that holds the ultimate moral good to be self-perfection, or human flourishing, and that the central intellectual virtue of such a way of life is *phronēsis* (practical wisdom) or prudence. Self-perfection, or flourishing, is in this view: (1) objective, (2) inclusive, (3) individualized, (4) agent-relative, (5) achieved with, and among, others, and (6) self-directed. Despite its classical source, this view is in many respects a newcomer to contemporary ethical discussion. Its combination of interrelated features generates a conception of the human good that has seldom been considered in its own right and certainly not with respect to liberalism. The foregoing features can be outlined as follows.

(1) According to this neo-Aristotelian approach, the end, or *telos*, of human life is the self-perfection of the individual human being. The attainment of this end requires that one live intelligently – that is, with some reflection upon who one is and the circumstances under which one acts. An intelligent life is not primarily a matter of employing intelligence or reason to achieve whatever one happens to desire. Rather this way of life comprehends the ends one needs to desire and thus involves the satisfaction of *right* desire. The satisfaction of right desire in turn constitutes what Aristotle called *eudaimonia* or what many philosophers now call 'human flourishing'.

Self-perfection or human flourishing is thus an objective good or value. Its basic or 'generic' constituents – for example, goods such as knowledge, health, friendship, creative achievement, beauty and pleasure, and virtues such as temperance, courage and justice – are determined by a consideration of human nature. However, the exact charac-

ter of these goods and role of these virtues are more complicated than
generally supposed, because flourishing, as we will see, also depends
on *who* as well as *what* we are and is not impersonal. As Aristotle states
when criticizing the Platonists, 'of honor, wisdom and pleasure, the
accounts are distinct and diverse. The good, therefore, is not some
common element answering to one idea' (*Nicomachean Ethics*
1096b 23–25); and as J. L. Ackrill notes:

> [Aristotle] certainly does think that the nature of man – the powers and
> needs all men have – determines the character that any satisfying human
> life must have. But since his account of the nature of man is in general
> terms the corresponding specification of the best life for man is also gen-
> eral. So while his assumption puts some limits on the possible answers to
> the question 'how shall I live?' it leaves considerable scope for a discussion
> which takes account of my individual tastes, capacities, and circumstances
> (Ackrill 1973).

So this interpretation of *eudaimonia* does not entail 'genericism' – that
is, the idea that all developmental processes are equivalent across individuals such that individuals come to be little more than repositories of
generic endowments. It is also for this reason that the universalist
propensities of modern ethical approaches such as utilitarianism and
deontologism are avoided.

Furthermore, human flourishing does not consist in the mere possession of the foregoing goods and virtues. Flourishing or living well is not
the same as having what it takes to live well. In fact, the basic or generic
goods would not exist as *goods* for human beings (or the virtues as
virtues) if they were not objects or manifestations of someone's effort. As
Aristotle points out, flourishing is an activity (*Nicomachean Ethics*, X,
6). If people are to flourish, they must direct themselves to the attainment
and coherent integration of these goods and virtues as best as circumstances will permit. Though self-perfection is an actuality, it is not a
static state. *Omne ens perficitur in actu*: flourishing is to be found in
action. The appropriateness of certain sorts of action is at least partly
determined in light of human nature.

(2) The flourishing of an individual human being is an 'inclusive' (as
opposed to 'dominant') end. Instead of there being one single dominant
end, which is the only thing of inherent worth and which makes everything else valuable only as a means, flourishing is conceived as being
constituted or defined by a number of virtues and goods, each of which
is valuable in its own right. Such virtues as integrity, courage and

justice, and such goods as friendship, creative achievement, health and knowledge, for example, are not only productive of flourishing, but expressive, and thus constitutive of it, as well. Thus it is possible for flourishing to be something sought for its own sake (a final end) without it trumping other goods or virtues in the process.

Since human flourishing is not some end that competes with such basic or generic goods as health, creative achievement, friendship and knowledge, it does not dominate and reduce their value to that of mere instruments. It recognizes the inherent worth of each and does not require a pre-set weighting or evaluative pattern of these constitutive ends. Weighting is thus something that is left to the individual to work out for himself, making *phronēsis*, or prudence, central to the achievement and maintenance of human flourishing.

Finally, moral virtues, for example, pride, courage, temperance and integrity, are not merely external means. Desires move us to action: towards objects of apparent benefit and away from objects of apparent harm. Yet our desires can be mistaken. If prudence is to succeed at the task of achieving, maintaining, enjoying and coherently integrating the multiple basic human goods in a manner that will be appropriate for us as the individuals we are, then the use and control of desires – that is, the creation of rational dispositions – is pivotal to flourishing. As rational dispositions, the moral virtues are expressions of human flourishing and are thus valuable in themselves.

(3) Just as our humanity is not some amorphous, undifferentiated universal, so human flourishing is not something abstract and universal. There is no such thing as 'human flourishing'; there is only individual human flourishing (Rasmussen and Den Uyl 1991, 63–4, 89–93). Abstractly considered, we can speak of human flourishing and of basic or generic goods and virtues; but concretely speaking no two cases of human flourishing are the same, and they are not interchangeable. One person's self-perfection is not the same as another's, any more than A's actualization of his potentialities is the same as B's actualization of his. There are individuative as well as generic potentialities, and this makes human fulfilment always something unique.

Individuals are more than loci at which human flourishing becomes spatially individuated. Human flourishing becomes real, achieves determinacy, only when the individual's unique talents, potentialities and circumstances are jointly employed. The human good does not exist apart from the choices and actions of individual human beings, nor does it exist independently of the particular mix of goods that individual human beings need to determine as being appropriate for their circumstances. The human good is individualized and diverse.

Since the specifics of these individually distinctive features of human flourishing are neither implied by, nor included in, an abstract account of human flourishing, the problem of balancing and prioritizing virtues cannot be solved in an *a priori* manner. An abstract consideration of human nature does not tell one what the proper relation should be of one virtue to the other virtues and goods. The proper mixture of the necessary elements of human flourishing cannot be read off human nature like one reads the Recommended Daily Allowances for vitamins and minerals off the back of a cereal box (Den Uyl 1991, 187–223).

Rather this is a task for prudence, and prudence occurs only through individuals confronting the contingent and particular facts of their concrete situation and determining at the time of action what in that situation may be truly good for them. This does not, however, mean either that one can with moral impunity ignore any of the necessary virtues or goods of human flourishing, or that one course of action in the concrete situation is as good as the next. Neither conventionalism nor subjectivism is implied. It simply means that ethical rationalism is false and that pluralism is morally appropriate.

(4) Human flourishing is agent-relative. Flourishing involves an essential reference to the person for whom it is good as part of its description. Abstractly stated, the human flourishing, G_1, for a person, P_1, is agent-relative if and only if its distinctive presence in world W_1 is a basis for P_1 ranking W_1 over W_2, even though G_1 may not be the basis for *any other* person's ranking W_1 over W_2. The best way to understand what this means, however, is to contrast it with its contradictory view, a view that considers basic values and reasons to be agent-neutral and ethics to be impersonal.

An ethical theory is impersonal when all ultimately morally salient values, reasons and rankings are 'agent-neutral'; and they are agent-neutral when they do *not* involve as part of their description an essential reference to the person for whom the value or reason exists or the ranking is correct. 'For any value, reason or ranking V, if a person P_1 is justified in holding V, then so are P_2-P_n under appropriately similar conditions... On an agent-neutral conception it is impossible to weight more heavily or at all, V, simply because it is one's own value' (Den Uyl 1991, 27). Accordingly, when it comes to describing a value, reason or ranking, it does not ethically matter whose value, reason or ranking it is. One person can be substituted for any other.

Using impersonal moral theory to make judgements and guide conduct requires that one consider only values, rankings and reasons that could be held by a rational agent, considered apart from all individuating conditions – be they natural, social or cultural. By adopting the perspective of such a rational agent, a person could never use some value crucial to *who* he or she is as a reason to give extra weight or importance to that value when determining the proper course of action.

For example, in this view the fact that course of action A results in assistance to one's own personal projects, family, friends or country, where non-A does not, provides no ethical reason for preferring A over non-A. These factors could perhaps explain how a person might feel about the situation, but when a person is acting from a properly moral perspective, considerations of a personal nature are irrelevant and should not weigh more heavily. The individual *qua individual* is not important in an impersonal moral theory The individual only represents a locus at which good is achieved or right conduct performed.

An impersonal ethics and an agent-neutral conception of basic values and reasons are, according to the version of neo-Aristotelian virtue ethics advanced here, unsound from root to branch. Particular and contingent facts are ethically important, and though some of these facts may be more important than others in achieving human moral well-being, this cannot be determined from the armchair. There is no great divide in the nature of things between the facts that can and cannot be ethically relevant.

Certainly there is no basis for holding that individual, social and cultural differences among people are ethically irrelevant. To the contrary, they are highly significant. Furthermore, there is no foundation to moral impersonalism's claim that values central to one's very conception of oneself may not be valued more than less central values. The fact that a value is crucial to some person's deeply held personal project, but to no one else's, does not make it morally irrelevant. In fact just the opposite is true. Such value deserves even more careful consideration, precisely because of its relation to oneself.

Further, it is fundamentally erroneous to assume that abstract ethical principles alone can determine the proper course of conduct. Such ethical rationalism fails to grasp that ethics is practical and contingent, and particular facts – which abstract ethical principles cannot *explicitly* capture and thus cannot be discovered *a priori* – are crucial to determining what ought to be done. Thus contrary to much of modern and contemporary ethics, not all morally proper forms of conduct need be universalizable.

In addition, and what is even more important, the central intellectual virtue of ethics is *phronēsis*. This is not, as we have already suggested, merely means–end reasoning, however. Rather it is the ability of the individual at the time of action to discern in particular and contingent circumstances just what is morally required. Without such a virtue, morality can only deal with ethical abstractions and not real questions of personal conduct and human life.

Finally, it should be emphasized that agent-relativity of values does not preclude them from being objectively and inherently valuable. That something is only valuable relative to some person does not necessarily make its value merely a matter of that person's attitude towards it – that is, merely something desired, wanted or chosen. Instead it can be valued, wanted, chosen because of what it objectively is. Also something can be an objective value that is an end in itself and nonetheless agent-relative. The constituent goods and virtues of human flourishing are, for example, inherently valuable but essentially related to the lives of individual human beings. But even more to the point, something can be not only agent-relative and *an* end in itself, but also *the* ultimate end or value, human flourishing itself.

As such, human flourishing is not something that competes with the good of individual human beings, but is the very fulfilment or flourishing of their lives. The ultimate objective and inherent value, the human *telos*,[28] just is their self-perfection or human flourishing. There is no flourishing-at-large. Flourishing is always the good-for-some-person. Thus it is perfectly consistent for the flourishing of individual human beings to be an objective and inherent value *and* essentially related to individual persons.[29] A commitment to the objectivity and inherent value of human flourishing does not imply that its value is something that can be exchanged or promoted regardless of whose flourishing it is. Agent-neutrality is not necessary for upholding value-objectivity or choice-worthiness.

(5) Human beings cannot flourish in isolation. Our fulfilment demands a life with others. We are social beings, not in the Hobbesian sense of merely needing others to get what we want because we are powerless on our own, but in the sense that our very maturation as human beings requires others. Indeed a significant part of our potentialities is other-oriented. This need to live with others must be expressed in some form but, considered abstractly, it can be expressed in any.

The specific form in which human sociality is expressed can be termed an 'exclusive relationship'. Exclusive relationships cover a continuum of relations – everything from close friends and confidants to business and work relations to mere acquaintances – but they all involve a principle of selectivity on the part of the participants in the relationship. It is through exclusive relationships that various types of groups, communities and even cultures are formed.

Since human flourishing is individualized, however, the way or manner in which the need for sociality is expressed is not limited to some select pool or group of humans. Though nearly everyone starts life within a family, a community, a society and a culture, this does not mean that one must be confined to only those relationships that constitute one's family, community, society or culture. The forms of human sociality are not necessarily limited or closed to any human being. Human sociality can involve the exploration of relationships with new and different people and varied ways of living, working and thinking.

This open-ended character of human sociality leads us to describe relationships that might develop as being 'non-exclusive'. No principle of selectivity is involved, for we are noting that human sociality, prior to a person's choice and selection, imposes no limitation regarding with whom and under what circumstances one may have a relationship. Further, non-exclusive relationships often provide the wider context in which exclusive relationships are formed, because many, if not most, exclusive relationships come about only because there was first a non-exclusive relationship. Thus human beings are social animals in the sense that, though there must be some set of exclusive relations through which one expresses one's sociality, there is no *a priori* exclusion of anyone from participation in those relations.

(6) The view of human flourishing that has been presented so far could correctly be described as entailing a 'pluralistic realism' regarding human values. The human good is something real, *and* it is individualized and diverse. Further, it is agent-relative. But there is something at the concrete level that is common to all the various forms of flourishing and, indeed, must be. As noted earlier, human flourishing is not only an actuality, it is an activity. It is an activity according to virtue, and the central virtue of human flourishing is practical wisdom – that is, *phronēsis*.

Yet practical wisdom is not passive. It is fundamentally a self-directed activity. The functioning of one's reason or intelligence, regardless of one's level of learning or degree of ability, is not something that occurs automatically. It requires individual effort. Effort is needed to initiate and maintain thought. In fact, effort is needed for reason to discover the goods and virtues of human flourishing as well as to achieve and implement them.

It is crucial to grasp that human reason (or intelligence) and self-directedness (or what might be loosely called 'autonomy') are not two separate faculties but distinct aspects of the same act. The act of reason, of exercising one's intellectual capacity, is an exercise of self-direction, and the act of self-direction is an exercise of reason. Thus self-perfection suitably describes the nature of the human good, because not only is *the object of perfection* the individual human being, *the agent of perfection* is the individual human being as well. Together they characterize the very nature of human flourishing.

Self-directedness is, then, both a necessary condition for self-perfection and a feature of all self-perfecting acts at whatever level of achievement or specificity. Yet this is another way of saying that the phenomenon of a volitional consciousness[30] is both a necessary condition for, and an operating condition of, the pursuit and achievement of self-perfection. The relationship between self-directedness and self-perfection can be summarized as follows: the absence of self-directedness implies the absence of self-perfection, although the absence of self-perfection does not imply the absence of self-directedness; nor does the presence of self-directedness imply the presence of self-perfection (but the presence of self-perfection does imply the presence of self-directedness).

None of this, of course, is to say that any choice one makes is as good as the next, but simply that the choice must be one's own and must involve considerations that are unique to the individual. One person's moral well-being cannot be exchanged with another's. The good-for-me is not, and cannot be, the good-for-you. Human moral well-being, then, is something objective, self-directed and highly personal. It is not abstract, collectively determined or impersonal.

While the foregoing account may outline the type of ethical framework we employ in thinking about liberalism, the metanormative structure of liberalism is first defined by individual rights. It is, therefore, the connection between this sort of general ethical structure and liberalism that interests us here. This connection is made through the language and medium of rights. A two-fold problem thus presents itself: (1) how are rights connected to this neo-Aristotelian ethical framework, and (2) how can rights be so connected and still imply a liberal social order when the opposite is more commonly asserted? We take it as given that the presence of the concept of rights is not *ipso facto* a sign that one is speaking of a liberal order.[31]

RIGHTS, ETHICS AND LIBERALISM

The most intractable struggles, political liberalism assumes, are
confessedly for the sake of highest things.

John Rawls, *Political Liberalism*

The individualized character of human flourishing creates a need for
another type of ethical principle, once we realize that human moral
well-being is only achieved with and among others. Sociality is an
inherent feature of our flourishing. We can only flourish with and
among others. This does not mean, however, that the particular social
and cultural forms in which our sociality is currently manifested exhaust the forms that can and should be taken. Our interpersonal relationships are not limited to only those with whom we share values.
They are open-ended. The interpersonal dimension of human flourishing allows for an openness to strangers and human beings in general. It
needs to be possible for persons in pursuit of their self-perfection to
have relationships with others with whom no common values are yet
shared and where all that is known is that one is dealing with another
human being.

If what has been said about our sociality is true, however, there is a
difficulty. If one person's particular form of well-being is different
from another's and may even conflict with it, and if persons can prevent
others from being self-directed, then certain interpersonal standards
need to be adopted if individuals are to flourish in their diverse ways
among others. Ordinary prescriptive norms would seem to fly in the
face of diversity by requiring conduct to be of a specific form or type.
An ethical principle is therefore needed whose primary function is not
guiding a person to well-being or right conduct, but providing a standard that favours no particular form of human flourishing, while at the
same time providing a context for its diverse forms. Such a principle
would seek to protect what is necessary to the possibility of each and
every person's finding fulfilment, regardless of the determinate form
virtues and human goods take in their lives. This sort of concept we
describe as being a metanormative principle, and we would claim that
basic rights, at least in liberal orders, are metanormative principles.

The problem of rights is a problem in liberalism itself, since rights
are the language through which liberalism is spoken. In the simplest
terms, the problem is how does one both recognize and provide for
plurality in human flourishing and also simultaneously give a moral

basis to one's civil order? Is not the choice one of abandoning morality for plurality or plurality for morality, or perhaps maximizing one against the other? Morality, in other words, would seem to call for a certain uniformity of conduct. Since people have diverse interests, values and conceptions of the good, uniformity would seem to come at the expense of diversity. Liberal political theory, then, must address the issue of pluralism, and this means more than acknowledging the existence of many views of the human good. It means grasping that the human good is plural and complex, not monistic and simple, and hence that pluralism is morally appropriate.

Traditionally, liberal rights theorists have tended to drift in the direction of solving the morality/plurality problem by upholding the primacy of the right over the good and viewing rights as totally independent of any consideration of human flourishing, consequences, circumstances, values, goals or interests. Rights so conceived have been generally construed as expressions of an impersonalist moral theory. We have, however, already seen some of the difficulties of such a theory and do not think that its ethical rationalism, particularly as illustrated in the use of the principle of universalizability, can be sustained. There are, however, two additional points to consider in this connection.

First, appealing to the principle of universalizability will not suffice as a solution to liberalism's problem of reconciling diverse forms of flourishing with moral uniformity, because the principle of universalizability does not: (a) solve value conflicts, or (b) prove that the human good is truly the same for each of us.

Just as the production of Fred's good is a reason for Fred to act, so is the production of Mary's good a reason for Mary to act. Fred cannot claim that his good provides him with a legitimate reason to act without acknowledging that Mary's good provides her with a legitimate reason to act. Agent-relative values thus can be universalized in this sense, but this form of universalization is obviously not sufficient to establish *common* values or a reason for other-regarding conduct among persons. The universalization of agent-relative goods does not show Fred's good to be Mary's good, or the production of Mary's good as providing Fred with a reason for action, or vice versa. Thus if Fred's good should conflict with Mary's, universalizability could not provide a way out of this conflict.

There is also a widespread tendency to confuse an objective value with universality. But this is an error. As Henry B. Veatch has observed:

If the good of X is indeed but the actuality of X's potentialities, then this is a fact that not just X needs to recognize, but anyone and everyone else as well. And yet given the mere fact that a certain good needs to be recognized, and recognized universally, to be the good of X, it by no means follows that X's good must be taken to be Y's good as well, any more than the actuality or perfection or fulfillment of X needs to be recognized as being the actuality or perfection of Y as well (Veatch 1990, 194).

It is not true that some thing or activity, call it G or G-ing, cannot be objectively good for anyone unless it is so for everyone.

Second, there is a fundamental difficulty that stands in the way of anyone who uses impersonal moral theory. The difficulty is simply that nothing can be said in reply to those who ask why they ought to be moral in an impersonal sense. Using 'ought' does not require the adoption of an agent-neutral view of values, reasons and rankings, because there is an agent-relative sense of 'ought' that can be used. There is, in other words, no self-contradiction in asking why one 'ought' to adopt an impersonal moral theory (and we mean here why it would be good, worthy or appropriate to do so). And since there is, *by definition*, no way that an impersonal moral theory can give a reason that is not an agent-neutral reason, it cannot provide an agent-relative reason why one should be moral in an impersonal sense. Any rights theory based on such an impersonal view of morality can provide neither reason nor motivation for moral conduct. This is a major, possibly insuperable, difficulty faced by anyone who bases the right to liberty on impersonal moral theory.

It is not necessary either to use impersonalist moral theory or adopt ethical rationalism in order to find a place for rights or a solution to liberalism's problem. The notion of human flourishing outlined above allows for the development of a conception of rights that is not reducible to other moral concepts, while at the same time being grounded in a personalist setting. We can best understand this by appreciating further the central role of self-directedness.

Self-direction is the exercise of practical reason, and this act of reason is present in every version of human flourishing, because it is that through which the individualization of human flourishing occurs. Without self-direction human flourishing would not be human flourishing. The protection of self-direction does not favour any form of human flourishing over any other, because it is the act of exercising practical reason that is being protected, not the achievement of its object. Further, self-direction is not amoral. Simply stated, one needs to exercise reason. It is good to do so; one ought to do so. Before ever addressing questions about what one should reason about or how one should conduct oneself, an analysis of the nature of human flourishing reveals that one should think and act for oneself, that is, be self-directed.

It is, of course, seldom the case that one ever confronts the issue of exercising one's reason or intelligence just as such. We reason about, pass judgement on and give priority to, some issue or object; and so this abstract point about the fundamental importance of self-direction to the nature of human flourishing is rarely faced in ethical conduct. Yet since neither speculative nor practical reason simply occurs 'naturally', the primary importance of self-direction becomes more apparent when abstracted from specific contexts and applied to politics.

The nature of political life forces us into the abstraction because we must look to that which applies to all. Since self-direction is not only common to, but required by, all forms of human flourishing (or their pursuit), regardless of the level of achievement or specificity, it is that unique feature of human flourishing that everyone must first have protected in the concrete instance if they are to flourish. A principle that provides for protection of self-directedness will not favour any particular form of flourishing, but will still allow the possibility that everyone can flourish.

We should not move too quickly here, however. Since the protection of self-directedness is central to the development of our theory of rights and thus crucial to our solution to liberalism's problem, the exact nature of the relation of self-directedness to practical wisdom, as well as to the other virtues and goods of human flourishing, bears repeating: practical wisdom cannot be practical wisdom without self-direction; and no constituent virtue or good of human flourishing can be such a virtue or good without practical wisdom. Thus self-directedness is both central and necessary to the very nature of human flourishing. It is the only feature of human flourishing common to all acts of self-perfection and peculiar to each. It expresses the fundamental core of human flourishing. Self-directedness is the only feature of human flourishing upon which to base a solution to liberalism's problem, because: (1) it is the only feature in which each and every person in the concrete situation has a necessary stake; and (2) it is the only feature of human flourishing whose protection is consistent with the diverse forms of human flourishing.

Rights are concerned with protecting the condition under which moral conduct – for us, self-perfection – can occur. Obviously, securing the basic condition for the possibility of self-perfection is logically prior to, and distinct from, the actual pursuit of self-perfection. But securing the condition must be understood as essentially 'negative'. This is because self-directedness does not imply or guarantee self-perfection and because one person's self-perfection is not exchangeable with another's. In other words, we are *not* trying with our theory of rights *directly* and *positively* to secure self-perfection, but rather to protect, and thus prevent encroachments upon, the condition under which self-perfection can exist. Our aim is thus to protect the possibility of self-perfection, but only through seeking to protect the possibility of self-directedness.

Because we are not directly concerned with the promotion of self-perfection itself, but only the condition for it, it is not the consequences *per se* that will determine encroachment. What is decisive is whether the action taken by one person towards another secures that other's consent or is otherwise in accord with that other's choices. One may violate another's rights and produce a chain of events that leads to consequences that could be said to be to that other's apparent or real benefit, or one may not violate another's rights and produce a chain of events that leads to one's apparent or real detriment.

Yet since the purpose here is to structure a political principle that protects the condition for self-perfection rather than the production of self-perfection itself, the consequences of actions are of little importance (except insofar as they threaten the condition that rights were designed to protect in the first place). Our concern here is not with how acts will turn out, but rather with setting the appropriate foundation for the taking of any action in the first place.

Thus though 'rights' are ethical principles, they are a special kind. Their function is *not* to provide persons with direct guidance in achieving good or conducting themselves properly. They are not normative principles, but are instead *metanormative* principles: that is to say, they concern the preconditions of moral conduct and arise because of the need to establish, interpret and evaluate political/legal contexts so that individuals can achieve their moral well-being in consort with others. Since the single most common and threatening encroachment upon self-directedness is the initiation of physical force by one person (or group) against another, rights – to borrow a phrase from Robert Nozick (Nozick 1974, 57) – allow 'moral space' to each person – a sphere of freedom whereby self-directed activities can be exercised without being trampled by others, or vice versa. Such is the right to liberty.

On the basis of what we have said so far, it should be clear that the only types of rights we possess that are consistent with protecting the condition necessary for the pursuit of any form of self-perfection are *rights of equal liberty*, where no one is allowed to take an action towards another that undermines the conditions required by that other's self-directedness. The basic rights we possess are thus principles of mutual non-interference. This translates socially into a principle of maximum compossible and equal freedom for all.[32]

The freedom must be equal, in the sense that it must allow for the possibility of diverse modes of flourishing and, therefore, must not be structurally biased in favour of some forms of flourishing over others. The freedom must be compossible, in the sense that the exercise of self-directed activity by one person must not encroach upon that of another. Thus a theory of rights that protects persons' self-directedness can be used to create a political/legal order that will not necessarily require that the flourishing of any person or group be sacrificed to any other.

If rights are metanormative principles that concern the basic structure of a civil order, how can they be said to provide any moral guidance to individuals? If one person murders another, for example, does not the one violate the other's rights, and is it not appropriate to say that one ought not to do such a thing? And if one is told not to do such a thing, is it not the case that an ordinary moral norm has been provided and that one is under an ordinary obligation to refrain from such actions? Further, would not one have this obligation irrespective of the presence of the state (as Locke suggested) in the sense of there being a *natural* right on the part of each of us against such actions?

At the risk of some repetition, it is important that we be clear about the status of rights in answering these questions. Rights are not normative principles in the sense of guiding us towards the achievement of our self-perfection. And contrary to appearances, they are not ordinary interpersonal normative principles either. Rights express the moral principle that must obtain if we are to reconcile our natural sociality with diverse forms of flourishing. We need, in other words, social life, but we also need to succeed as individuals approaching a particular form of flourishing. Norms which specify how to live among others and the obligations one is likely to incur in such a life are one thing; norms which define the setting for such interactions and obligations are quite another. The 'obligations' one has to another in the latter case are due to a shared need to act in an orderly social/political context.

The obligations one has in the former case are a function of what is needed to live well and cannot be generated apart from the particular actions, context, culture, traditions, intentions and practices in which one finds oneself acting. These actions and contexts call forth evaluative norms by which success, propriety and merit can be measured and judged in particular cases. Metanorms (rights) are not, however, *called* upon by the progress of a culture or individual, but rather *depended* upon. From our perspective, then, it is likely that something multifaceted is taking place in the example where one person 'murders' another.

At one level, the person's 'natural' rights are being violated. That is, by our nature as social and diverse creatures, the action in question is not suited to setting an appropriate context for human flourishing; nor does it seem likely that it will be conducive to actual progress towards flourishing itself. The latter aspect, however, is very much tied up with moral elements besides those needed to set a basic context (for example, considerations of country, family, friends, fellow citizens, the law, and so on). The moral norms at work here presuppose an environment where moral conduct is possible. In addition, these norms specify the sort of conduct that will be considered appropriate or worthy or justified. In the case of basic 'natural' rights, by contrast, the obligations are not so much to individuals *per se*, because such rights are fashioned independently of particular practices, circumstances and agents. The norms for basic rights apply to no one in particular and to everyone equally at all times.

In this respect, the standard sort of 'state of nature' analysis may actually confuse the issue, rather than help clarify it. We are tempted to abandon the social and ask what one would be obligated to do if there were no law, society, culture or political authority around one to define any duties. If one person does injury to another in such a state of nature, it looks as though only one level of obligation is present, since by definition there is no particular society or political context to offer any other. The normative and metanormative seem to collapse into the single duty of respecting another's natural rights. Securing the setting (non-interference), in other words, appears to be the same as undertaking appropriate conduct itself.

It may be, of course, that we are obliged to take some actions because of their necessary connection to achieving an appropriate context for ourselves and others. In this respect, metanormative obligations would be no less important and binding than any others. But injuring another in a state of nature recalls more than simply signifying conduct in violation of actions needed to secure and maintain the appropriate conditions for flourishing in a social context. Such an action calls forth a whole normative tradition about the proper treatment of persons. This is fine provided we distinguish the metanormative from the normative elements. But a state of nature analysis does not allow us to do this well. Murder, for example, is usually defined by particular social, political and cultural contexts. To abandon these for the state of nature gives us the illusion that society is only marginally relevant to a determination of what will count as murder and that *all* norms are context-setting norms (for example, rights).

Individuals must, therefore, respect the natural rights of others not because they will be better persons or be 'doing the right thing', but because their very ability to act *jointly* as persons depends upon securing the conditions necessary for such action. A state of nature approach may help us identify those metanormative principles, but it does next to nothing towards generating the normative rules or obligations that are equally necessary for a life of moral excellence. For that, one needs actors in concrete social settings. Consequently, if the metanormative conditions are threatened or destroyed (for example, by a Nazi takeover), the language of natural rights would not be inappropriate. It is both right by nature (that is, by appeal to human nature) that a certain context for human action be secured and a *right* (in the sense of a claim about a certain sort of treatment due one) that one not be treated in certain ways *in light of what is necessary to secure that context.*[33]

What one cannot do is pretend that when one refers to 'murder' in a state of nature the reference is devoid of any conception of social life. The full horror of a violation of someone's 'natural rights' comes precisely because one has an idea of how human beings should treat each other, both in civilized society and with respect to what it takes to establish such a society. Our point here, then, is that state of nature analysis is usually parasitical upon civilization.[34] No one could disseminate Hobbes's rules for peace (as found in Chapter XV of *Leviathan*) who was unfamiliar with civilized life.[35]

Part of the problem we are addressing arises because we are under the illusion that we can imagine ourselves as asocial beings. Asocial beings might worry about why they have any obligations at all towards others. One would then have to conjure up arguments as to why it might be in someone's interest to respect another's 'rights'. Social beings, by contrast, would never have a radical worry about why they should concern themselves with others because they come, as it were, already concerned.

A social being, in other words, is not likely to wonder why he or she should be concerned about setting the context for their own flourishing. We do not deny the heuristic value of state of nature thought experiments, but, with Aristotle, we do deny their value as a fundamental platform for moral analysis and understanding. In any case, liberalism *per se* does not require the radicalized version of such an approach (where morality itself is generated by a 'contract'); and it is arguable in most cases whether the fathers of liberalism (for example, Locke and even Hobbes) saw the moral as exclusively derived from the state of nature.

Liberalism's problem, in any case, can be put another way: how can liberalism retain any connection to a substantive moral philosophy and demand so little politically? We need not repeat the account given in chapter 2 in response to this question. All that needs to be noted here is that the preceding theory retains a strong connection with a substantive moral position (the Aristotelian) without lapsing into a moralistic politics. Liberalism can not afford to close off the path to a rich moral posture any more than it can still remain a liberalism while politically dictating a particular form of moral living. There are those, however, who claim that liberalism cannot succeed either in remaining uncommitted to particular forms of flourishing or to a substantive ethics. To such issues we now turn.

4. Analyses and Objections

THE CHALLENGE OF LIBERAL COMMUNITARIANISM

> Recognition of a pluralism of forms of human flourishing, each objective, of which only some can exist in a liberal regime, destroys the authority of liberalism as a universal, trans-historical and cross-cultural ideal.
>
> John Gray, *Post-Liberalism: Studies in Political Thought*

John Gray is a post-liberal, for he does not think that it is any longer plausible to claim that liberty is a universal human value. He is also a communitarian, because he thinks that the attempt to find a *theoretical* basis upon which to ground liberal political philosophy is doomed. According to Gray, the liberal form of civil society only survives and prospers because of our commitment to it. This commitment is manifested in the realm of practice and is not fully theorizable. Thus when it comes to determining the meaning, scope and validity of liberty, neither political nor jurisprudential theory is adequate. Such determinations are provided only by a form of political reasoning that is essentially circumstantial. Consequently, the political has primacy over the theoretical and legal. Further, though Gray is sympathetic to aspects of neo-Aristotelian virtue ethics, he is quite sure that such an ethics cannot employ a meaningful notion of perfection as an adequate foundation for liberalism's claim that liberty is a universal political value.

The basic reason for Gray's abandoning liberalism, adopting a communitarian perspective and rejecting the very idea of perfection can be summed up in two words: value pluralism. Or maybe it would be more accurate to say, Gray's *understanding* of value pluralism, for it will be with his understanding of it and with what he claims flows from it that we will take issue.

Gray makes it very clear that value pluralism is not ethical relativism, be it in either conventionalist or subjectivist form. Nor is it moral scepticism. Rather it is a species of moral realism that Gray calls 'objective pluralism'. Thus there is moral knowledge; there are real goods, values and excellences. However, they are diverse, irreducible and incommensurable – with nothing that necessarily unifies them. Indeed they are so radically plural that rational choice is limited. We often face moral dilemmas for which there is no way to avoid doing wrong or suffering an irreplaceable loss of value.

As a result of this pluralism, liberal rights are not uniquely legitimate for all human beings. There have been human beings who have flourished in regimes that are not liberal, and there are forms of human flourishing that are driven out by liberal regimes. Overall, there is no single, determinate way of life that is right or best for all human beings. Thus Gray concludes that liberalism cannot use the notion of perfection to justify its claim to offer liberty as a universal political value.

Gray's claims and charges are complex. We need to be very clear about exactly what he means by 'objective pluralism'. The following two statements by Gray, the first from 'What is dead and what is living in liberalism?' (Gray 1993, 291) and the second from 'Agonistic liberalism' (Gray 1995, 116) are worth quoting at length:

> *Objective pluralism* of this sort affirms that ultimate values are knowable; that they are many; that they often conflict and are uncombinable, and that there is no overarching standard whereby their claims are rationally arbitrable: there are conflicts among the incommensurables. The diversity of ultimate values, great as it is, is not infinite; it is bounded by the limits of human nature. 'Incompatible these ends may be; but their variety cannot be unlimited, for the nature of men, however various and subject to change, must possess some generic character if it is to be called human at all.' This pluralism, bounded as it is, may come in several varieties, and may operate at several levels. Within the moral code of a particular culture, there may be lacunae that generate dilemmas which neither the code itself, nor the practical reasonings of the individual, can resolve. Hence are generated the radical or tragic courses among competing evils or rival excellences, in which whatever is chosen entails some great loss or irreparable wrong ... Also, there is the variety of pluralism which illuminates value conflict, not within cultures or individuals, but between cultures or whole forms of life having incommensurable values as constitutive elements. These varieties of pluralism may interpenetrate one another, especially when (as in the late modern world) cultures and forms of life have come to interact deeply with one another, are no longer easily individuated, so that many individuals find themselves (in Fulke Greville's phrase) 'suckled on the milk of many nurses', formed by many distinct cultural traditions.

> [T]here is an irreducible diversity of ultimate values (goods, excellences, options, reasons for action, and so forth) and that when these values come

into conflict or competition with one another there is no overarching standard or principle, no common currency or measure, whereby such conflicts can be arbitrated or resolved ... Value pluralism imposes limits on rational choice that are subversive of most standard moral theories, not merely utilitarianism, and it has deeply subversive implications for all the traditional varieties of liberal theory. In particular, it has the implications that we often face practical and moral dilemmas in which reason leaves us in the lurch and in which, whatever we do, there is a wrong or irreplaceable loss of value. Value pluralism implies that the fundamental rights or basic liberties of liberal thought cannot be insulated from conflicts among incommensurables.

We can note right away that objective pluralism carries with it a rejection of two classical ethical beliefs: (1) that the human good is a single, common form, a monistic whole, with no intrinsic constituents that are irreducible and valuable in themselves; and (2) that all the goods and virtues that constitute the human good are in principle harmonious, with only lack of sufficient knowledge or moral commitment preventing their unification. Instead the goods and virtues that constitute human flourishing are often incompatible, and there is no overarching standard whereby conflicts among these goods or combinations of them might be solved – that is, these goods (or combinations of them) are incomparable and incommensurable. They are incomparable because there is no relevant respect in which one may be judged in relation to another, and they are incommensurable because there is no scale of reference in which one may be judged higher or lower than the other. Thus there are many irreducible values, which are valuable in themselves, that are incompatible, incomparable and incommensurable.

Incommensurability is, however, even more extensive. Values are integrated within cultural and social wholes; they belong to the form of life which generates them. Thus incommensurability can occur not only within cultures and individuals, but also, 'when goods, virtues, and excellences are elements in whole ways of life that depend on uncombinable social structures as their matrices' (Gray 1995, 118). Incommensurability can thus be found between cultures or whole forms of life. This form of incomparability and lack of a common measure is possibly the fullest expression of the value-conflict generated by objective pluralism.

Gray holds that objective pluralism is destructive of the very idea of perfection. It:

strikes a death-blow at the classical foundation of our culture, expressed not only in Plato and Aristotle, but in the Stoic idea of the *logos* and in

Aquinas's conception of a world order that was rational and moral in essence, even as it was the creation of the Deity, one of the central attributes of which was perfection (Gray 1993, 291).

It is not merely that human beings cannot achieve perfection; rather it is that the very idea of perfection makes no sense.

'Human flourishing' remains, however, valid for Gray, because it is reconceptualized. It still consists of more than mere subjective preferences or desires and encompasses the use of human capacities that are reflectively judged as worthwhile, but it is now non-hierarchical. Incommensurability precludes objective rankings or weightings of ultimate values. No one form of life – say, the life of rational inquiry, of contemplation, of wealth creation, of prayer or selfless devotion to others – is the best for the human species. The virtues are not necessarily unified; and the conflicts among goods or excellences, many of which are neither comparable nor commensurable, reveal that there is no uniquely rational combination of them. Indeed the variety of incommensurable forms of human flourishing is so radically underdetermined by the generic powers and capacities of human beings that it must be frankly acknowledged that human beings are partly self-creators over time and in history.

Gray takes this objective pluralism as having fatal implications for liberal political philosophy (Gray 1995, 119–120). Two of these we need to consider here. First, the structure of basic liberties or the content of fundamental rights is massively underdetermined by any general ethical theory. Gray agrees with Raz that rights are not foundational. Rather they are intermediaries between claims about human interests that are vital to human flourishing and claims about what obligations are reasonable to impose upon others in respect of those interests; and since there are different forms of human flourishing which spawn different judgements of human interest and, thereby, of the weights or values of rival liberties, there is no uniquely rational way to solve conflicts of liberties. Rights claims cannot be sealed off from the effects of objective pluralism.

Second, hard cases abound because of the conflicts among rights and liberties that express incompatible, incomparable and incommensurable values. These hard cases, which are undecidable by reasoning from any overarching theory, are the rule, not the exception. Accordingly no right answers to hard cases about what constitutes restraint of liberty can be provided at the theoretical or jurisprudential level. Rather answers can only be provided at the political level through a form of practical reasoning in which no step is necessitated.

Politics is, therefore, an autonomous sphere of practical life with primacy over the theoretical and legal:

> This way of treating questions about the restraint of liberty appeals to a conception of political life as a sphere of practical reasoning whose *telos* is a *modus vivendi*, to a conception of the political in which it is a domain devoted to the pursuit not of truth but of peace – an approach that has the authority of Hobbes (Gray 1995, 122).

However, the thinker whose conception of political life best conforms to Gray's position is not Hobbes, for Hobbes is too much of a rationalist. Rather, as Gray notes, it is Machiavelli. It is Machiavelli's cardinal achievement, according to Isaiah Berlin, to have recognized that ends, 'equally ultimate, equally sacred, may contradict each other; [and] that entire systems of value may come into collision without possibility of rational arbitration, and not merely in exceptional circumstances, as a result of abnormality or accident or error ... but as part of the normal human situation' (Berlin 1982, 74–5).

Though there is more that can be said about Gray's own version of liberalism, our first concern is with his account of objective pluralism and its implications for a self-perfectionist virtue ethics and the view of rights that we base upon it. Beginning with Gray's account of objective pluralism, we can see many features that coincide with our view of human flourishing.

These are as follows: that human flourishing is not a single dominant good or excellence – a monistic whole – but is, instead, composed of many goods and excellences that are valuable in themselves; that there is no one single combination or weighting of goods and excellences that can be 'read off' an abstract account of human flourishing and taken as the best for human beings (the first classical view mentioned above); that an ethical rationalism that tries to determine *a priori* for someone what is good and ought to be done in the concrete situation is inadequate; that the number and variety of the goods and excellences that constitute human flourishing are not infinite; that there is generic content to the notion of human flourishing which, though it must be fleshed out by individual and cultural considerations, is not merely a place-holder whose content is determined entirely by communal practices and traditions; and, accordingly, that ethical relativism – be it subjectivism or conventionalism – is not true.

The major difference between objective pluralism and our conception of human flourishing concerns the implications of agent-relativity. Gray believes that if one holds an agent-relative conception of basic or ultimate value, then such value can be neither inherent nor objective. Agent-relativity requires denying inherent value to various forms of human flourishing and endorsing ethical relativism (Gray 1993, 309). Thus, perfection cannot be, as it is for us, individualized, agent-relative, and self-directed. Rather, it has to be universal, agent-neutral, and cosmic. We hold, for reasons already presented, that agent-relativity does not require denying inherent value or objectivity to versions of human flourishing. Nor does it imply ethical relativism. This difference is crucial, because it goes to the very heart of Gray's claim that the idea of perfection is incoherent.

If perfection is agent-relative and individualized (the self-directed character of perfection will be discussed later), then Gray's claim that versions of human flourishing (that is, combinations, patterns or weightings of generic goods and virtues) are incomparable and incommensurable is either pointless or not the problem he supposes it to be for ethics – at least, that is, for the virtue ethics we have been advancing. Thus Gray's attack on the concept of perfection is undercut. We will examine this issue in some detail.

Versions of human flourishing are incommensurable when two conditions are fulfilled: when neither is better than the other, that is, they are incomparable, and when another version of human flourishing is better than one of the other two valuable forms of flourishing but not better than the other. This is a breakdown in transitivity in practical reasoning and the basis for Gray's claim that objective pluralism destroys the very idea of perfection: 'Incommensurability ... is the radical denial of the very meaning of perfection' (Gray 1995, 117). However, if we are to speak of versions of flourishing that are more or less valuable, we must consider the question: 'valuable to whom?' We cannot assess the significance of Gray's claims unless we first answer this question.

If we assume that human flourishing involves no essential reference to the person for whom it is valuable as part of its description, and that individuals are no more than loci for instantiations of human flourishing, then pointing out that there are versions of human flourishing that are incomparable and incommensurable has a point. It shows the error in believing that practical reasoning requires everyone in the same situation to hold the same valuation, reason and ranking regarding a certain version of human flourishing. It also shows the error of 'genericism' – that is, the error of assuming that all developmental processes are equivalent across individuals, such that individuals come to be little more than repositories of generic endowments.

Incomparability creates a problem, and incommensurability arises for versions of flourishing only if it is assumed that the individual is ethically irrelevant to determining the value and character of a given form of flourishing. There is a breakdown in transitivity in practical reasoning primarily because it is assumed that the aim of ethics is to provide a set of specific, impersonal, equally suited rules of conduct for everyone instead of providing individual guidance. Incomparability and incommensurability do, indeed, destroy the idea of perfection for those who see flourishing as a manifestation of a universal order or cosmic *logos*.

But if perfection is realized in an agent-relative, individualized, self-directed manner, then the destruction Gray sees as following in the wake of incomparable and incommensurable versions of human flourishing is not so evident. Indeed, if human flourishing involves an essential reference to the person for whom it is valuable as part of its description, and if the individual provides relevant content to the character of human flourishing, then pointing out that there are versions of human flourishing that are incomparable creates no problem. This is entailed by the claim that human flourishing is both agent-relative and individualized. There is no version of human flourishing that is better or more valuable than some other version *period*; versions of human flourishing are only valuable *relative* to some person. Thus if we are careful not to confuse abstractions with realities, we see that one person's version of human flourishing is not strictly comparable with another's. The pursuit and achievement of human flourishing is not a race in which everyone competes for the same prize; there is no unified race, with a single standard for swiftness. Instead each person must himself run according to a standard of swiftness that is linked to that person's successful completion of a race against *dysdaimonia* (unhappiness or lack of flourishing).

Could a person, after considering what we call his 'nexus' – that is, the set of circumstances, talents, endowments, interests, beliefs and histories that descriptively characterizes him and which he brings to any new situation – discover that there is more than one combination, pattern or weighting of generic goods and virtues that are equally valuable for him? This is possible. Yet it does not follow that there are no parameters or limits on choice. Practical reason is not destroyed. A consideration of generic goods and virtues imposes some limitations. For example, could anyone reasonably claim to flourish if they neither had nor sought friends; had no integrity, courage or justice; let their passions run wild or repressed all emotions; or cared nothing for knowledge, reason, consistency or truth? Is not Socrates dissatisfied better than a fool satisfied?

There are also limits imposed by one's own nexus. For example, one might wish for a career as a venture capitalist, but the solidified components of one's nexus structurally identify one as an academic. Of course it may be possible to structure both, but a life such as that would be difficult to manage, requiring more than the ordinary amount of practical wisdom. In any case, simply because there is more than one version of human flourishing that is right for a person at a certain time does not mean that such will be the case at another time. The possibilities open to a 20-year-old will not necessarily be open to a person of 60; and this is so not just because of ageing, but also because of the choices one has made.

Through choices, one combines components of one's life into an identity, and these choices over time limit the range of future choices. None of these choices is made *a priori*, however. Time and circumstance are crucial, and so they serve to limit choice also. Though the forms of human perfection are much greater and standards more flexible than some ethical rationalists or classical natural law theorists ever imagined, perfection is still something that can be intelligently pursued.

Yet could not Gray argue that if there are agent-relative, individualized versions of human flourishing that are incomparable, then there could also be versions that are incommensurable? As long as human flourishing is viewed in an agent-neutral manner and the input of the individual ignored, this contention has plausibility. When considered as a claim regarding agent-relative, individualized versions of human flourishing, however, it is dubious. Again we should be clear about what this claim means. It would mean that there are two versions of human flourishing that are equally valuable to some person *and* that there is another version that is more valuable than one of the other two versions to that person, but not more valuable than the other to that person. However, what would be the basis for claiming such incommensurability? Since human flourishing is both agent-relative and individualized, it is not clear how we get from the diversity, or even incomparability, of forms of human flourishing to their incommensurability.

If A and B are two forms of human flourishing that are equally valuable to an individual, and if C is a more valuable form of flourishing to that individual than A, what basis is there for saying that C is not also more valuable to that individual than B? Gray wants to say that the world is such that someone's practical reasoning could be intransitive but not due to any failure of knowledge or moral commitment. Gray rejects subjectivism, conventionalism and scepticism in ethics and has agreed that there is some generic character to our understanding of human flourishing; so he is not simply a nominalist. On what, then, could the claim of incommensurability among agent-relative, individualized versions of human flourishing be based? Since Gray never considers the effects of such a view of human flourishing on his charge that there are versions of human flourishing that are incommensurable, he provides no answer to this question.

There is, however, a dimension of Gray's thought which we have mentioned but have not yet considered in determining the alleged effects of incommensurability on the concept of perfection. This is the idea that goods and virtues are integrated into social wholes. Gray claims that when goods and virtues are elements in whole ways of life that depend for their origin and development on social structures that are uncombinable, incommensurability occurs among forms of life and cultures. Further, there is a communitarian side to Gray's view of human beings. He understands human identity in terms of participation in common forms of life, and he means by this concrete historical practices that constitute actual communities, not ideal-typical abstractions. So it seems that incompatible social structures limit not only our ability rationally to compare and evaluate goods and virtues, but indeed our very understanding of what it is to be human.

There is, nonetheless, an ambiguity with this dimension of Gray's thought. Is it the case that human flourishing is actually defined and constituted by the concrete historical practices that make up communities and that there is nothing across cultures and over time in virtue of which we may speak of *human* flourishing? Gray seems at times to be answering this question in the affirmative. Yet it should be recalled that Gray is insistent that objective pluralism not be interpreted as any form of ethical relativism or as moral scepticism: 'If value pluralism is correct, then these are *truths*, correct moral beliefs about the world. The thesis of incommensurability of values is then not a version of relativism, of subjectivism, or of moral skepticism' (Gray 1995, 118).

Thus it cannot be the case for Gray that cultural and social traditions of a given community constitute or define human flourishing. They may be necessary conditions, but they are not necessary and sufficient. Similarly, human beings are most definitely social animals; they live in community with others and cannot be properly understood if this feature of their identities is ignored. However, this is not to say that what it is to be human is exhaustively accounted for by one's sociality, or that there is no sense to the term 'human' that is generic and can be used to locate human beings across cultures and over time.

Gray accepts the idea that there is some generic character to being human: 'The nature of men, however, various and subject to change, must possess some generic character if it is to be called human at all' (Gray 1993, 291).[36] Consequently, it would be wrong to say, according to Gray, that because human flourishing and humanity are always culturally and socially specific, they are also culturally and socially bound. In other words, it would be wrong to claim that the validity of a generic account of human flourishing or the adequacy of a generic description of human being is limited to a certain culture or society and cannot be valid or adequate across cultures and times.

If ethical relativism is rejected by objective pluralism and generic features of human nature acknowledged, then versions of human flourishing are to that extent comparable and measurable. It is possible for communities as well as individuals to have conceptions of human flourishing that are wrong or not as well developed as others. As we said earlier, could anyone reasonably claim to flourish if they neither had nor sought friends, had no integrity, courage or justice; let their passions run wild or repressed all emotions; or cared nothing for knowledge, reason, consistency or truth? Is not Socrates dissatisfied better than a fool satisfied? Individuals and their forms of life can be generically compared and evaluated.

Nonetheless, it remains true that accounts of generic goods and virtues do not take us very far. They are not sufficient to make human flourishing something determinate or valuable, let alone provide much guidance. As David L. Norton observed so perceptively:

> When Mill says, 'It is better to be Socrates dissatisfied than a fool satisfied,' we must once again ask, 'For whom?' And we reject the answer implied by Mill, 'For everyone' ... Certainly it is better for Socrates to be Socrates. But for Mill to be Socrates (or try to be, since the proposal construes an impossibility) is distinctively worse than for Mill to be Mill, and correspondingly for you and for me.

> Pleasures are not objective, intrinsic good, distributable like horses to which we shall hitch our wagons. As conceived abstractly they are valueless, acquiring value or disvalue accordingly as the desires they reflect are commensurate or incommensurate with the persons whose desires they are (Norton 1976, 219).

Likewise, other generic goods (pleasure is, after all, a generic good) and virtues become actual and valuable – their proper combination, pattern or weighting is achieved – only in relation to individual human beings and their social and cultural situation. Consequently, incomparability among such combinations, patterns or weightings – whether its origin be due to individual, social or cultural differences – creates a problem of incommensurability only if it is assumed that these differences are ethically irrelevant because the determination of the value and character of generic goods and virtues must accord with some single pattern that is best for everyone. As said before, the incommensurability that is manifested in a breakdown in transitivity in practical reasoning arises primarily because it is assumed that the aim of ethics is to provide a set of specific, equally suited rules of conduct for all persons, regardless of their nexus and social/cultural situation. We, of course, reject this form of ethical rationalism.

It might yet be that the real problem for the view of human flourishing we have been advancing in this essay is neither incomparability nor incommensurability, but rather incompatibility. If human flourishing is an inclusive end, and if it is individualized and agent-relative, what leads us to believe that all the possible components necessary for a self-perfecting life can be made compossible? Gray points out many ways in which there could be conflict among the components of human flourishing – conflict occasioned, he contends, not by contingencies, but by the very natures of the goods and virtues that provide generic content to human flourishing. He notes, for example, that:

> A person with the virtues of courage, resolve, resourcefulness, intrepidity, and indominatability is unlikely to possess the virtues of modesty and humility ... [and] if Van Gogh had passed through successful psychoanalysis, he would have been a calmer soul, but it is hard to see how he could have painted as he did ... [S]ome human powers may depend for their exercise on weaknesses, lacks, or disabilities' (Gray 1993, 301–2).

These observations might be the most devastating of Gray's arsenal of objections against a self-perfectionist, virtue ethics.

Much needs to be said in response to this challenge, but there are two basic levels of response: an abstract level and a concrete level. At the abstract level, there is no logical connection between there being a plurality of ends that compose human flourishing and these ends being incompatible. It is not clear, in other words, that Gray has shown the natures of the generic goods and virtues to be the source of incompatibility. It seems rather, that incompatibility would only be likely to arise if we assume genericism, that is, if we assume that these goods and virtues are equal among themselves and identical across individuals.

It is when emphasis and unequal weighting are precluded from a conception of human flourishing that there is a high probability of conflict. Our view of human flourishing, on the contrary, accepts emphasis and unequal weighting as central to its very identity. Thus conflicts are not as likely because some goods and virtues need not, given a person's nexus and circumstances, be emphasized or weighted as highly as other goods and virtues. Determining the proper emphasis or weighting of goods and virtues is the task of *phronēsis*, and this is done at the concrete level.[37]

It is at the concrete level, in other words, that the coherence among a person's generic goods and virtues is either achieved or not. It is precisely the role of the virtue of *phronēsis* to keep one's ends from becoming incompatible. Its central task consists in achieving, maintaining, enjoying and coherently integrating these ends. This involves not only a continual monitoring of the 'fit' between generic goods and capacities and one's nexus, but also a consideration of those personal truths that apply only to oneself and serve to set standards for what is appropriate. *Phronēsis* involves intelligent management at all three levels at once. It is through this process that one finds a version of human flourishing appropriate for oneself.

Whether the goods and virtues that constitute human flourishing can be made compatible for someone is, then, not determinable *a priori*. Rather it is achieved only by the individual, at the time of action, confronting personal truths and considering contingent circumstances. It is therefore not possible for Gray to sustain his claim that the very nature of the goods and virtues that compose human flourishing leads to conflict. This has to be considered in each person's case. None of this is to say, however, that there cannot be human tragedies, that is, situations that, through no fault of the person, make it impossible for crucial goods and virtues to be integrated or terrible evils avoided.

Tragedies and disease do not seem, however, to be the norm, despite Gray's claims to the contrary. Nor does it seem necessary to endorse a providential conception of nature to say this. Rather one can simply point to the success of insurance companies in betting against disaster and disease. And even if the world were full of conflict and disappointment, that may only indicate the absence of prudence, not the presence of incompatibility.

It may be that we have not presented Gray's objection accurately. He may not be claiming that the generic goods and virtues of human flourishing lead to conflict, but that there are many goods in their concrete form that are constitutively incompatible, and that these goods cannot all be coherently combined into a single form of human flourishing. Gray notes the incompatibility of a priest's avocation with a soldier's virtues or a nun with the excellences of a courtesan.

But there is a confusion here of the concrete with the abstract. Certain specific concrete forms of virtue – the charity and courage of a priest and a soldier, respectively, or the nun's chastity and the courtesan's sexual sensitivity – may indeed not be combinable into a single form of flourishing, because elements of each person's nexus prevent it. This is what it means to say that human flourishing is individualized and not exchangeable. However, it does not follow that the generic virtues of charity and courage, or elements of chastity (for example, lack of promiscuity) and sexual sensitivity, could not be coherently combined in some other version of human flourishing that is appropriate for some person.

Indeed, it is a sign of personal maturity, if not flourishing, that one is able to recognize what is and is not suited to one's mode of life. Moreover, ethics does not require wishful thinking, where all forms of endeavour are open to one at all times. The virtues and goods which all seem equal in the abstract must take on particular forms in the concrete. It is neither possible for, nor the purpose of, ethics to dictate or anticipate every permutation (see Den Uyl 1991, 166–81; Rasmussen and Den Uyl 1991, 19–30).

The vacillation between generic considerations and concrete versions of human flourishing brings us to a rather curious feature of Gray's argument – namely his acceptance of the Enlightenment view of ethical reasoning. Despite his criticisms of the Enlightenment tendency to give theoretical reason (whose concern is for the universal and necessary) priority over practical reason (whose concern is for the contingent and particular), he nonetheless continues to accept this prioritization when evaluating ethical theories. Gray regards the inability of an ethical theory to provide universal, impersonal rules for social management as evidence of the limitation of reason in ethics and the primacy of radical choice. He correctly notes that human flourishing is individualized and that ethical rationalism does not suffice, but he too quickly accepts the counsel of despair and the limits of reason. He does not consider the possibilities that a virtue ethics of self-perfection is by definition not concerned with providing such rules, that the principle of universalizability is not the *sine qua non* of ethical reasoning, and that the ethical standards employed by normative ethics are not the same as those employed by political philosophy.

As should be clear, we do not accept the Enlightenment view of ethical reasoning, because human flourishing is individualized as well as agent-relative. For us, ethics requires the faculty of practical reason, and *phronēsis* (practical wisdom) is the excellent or virtuous use of this faculty. *Phronēsis* is more than the mere mechanical application of universal moral principles to concrete cases. It is intellectual insight that discovers in contingent and particular facts what is truly good for someone and thus what at the time of action ought to be done. Practical wisdom is, then, the intellectual virtue by which human flourishing becomes determinate and real. This form of reasoning does not aim at uniform directives that apply to any and everyone and should not be expected to provide standards that can be directly and positively employed in political philosophy. Thus the types of principle employed by normative ethics and by political philosophy are not, as Gray assumes, the same.

Before examining the consequences of Gray's objective pluralism for liberal political theory, Gray's view of self-direction or autonomy remains to be considered. Gray agrees with Joseph Raz that the absence of choice or self-direction does not diminish the value of human relations or displays of excellence. He approvingly quotes Raz: 'I do not see that the absence of choice diminishes the value of human relations or the displays of excellence in technical skills, physical ability, spirit and enterprise, leadership, scholarship, creativity or imaginativeness' (Raz 1989, 1227 cited in Gray 1993, 308).

Gray and Raz hold that all of these excellences can be encompassed in lives in which the pursuits and options of persons are not subject to individual choice. Self-direction is thus not an essential ingredient of every form of human flourishing. Rather the value of self-direction is a 'local affair'. Gray contends that:

> It is left open whether a form of life in which autonomy is inconspicuous or lacking – the form of life of medieval Christendom, or of feudal Japan in the Edo period – may be better from the standpoint of flourishing, or else simply incommensurably different, by comparison with the form of life of autonomous individuals (Gray 1993, 308).

Yet what does it mean for human beings to display excellence in technical skills, physical ability, spirit and enterprise, leadership, scholarship, creativity or imaginativeness? Are these excellences abstract, uniform and unrelated to the individual person? Are they merely excellent in some generic way? The answer to these questions must, of course, be 'no'. Excellence is found in the appropriate performance of these activities in a concrete situation, and what is appropriate is determined only in relation to the individual human being.

Further, the individual does more than merely instantiate some 'abstract' excellence. Rather these excellences must be appropriately individualized if they are to be determinate and valuable. One must incorporate them into one's nexus of excellences by an act of reason, and this is the task of the rational insight that is *phronēsis*. But this rational insight requires effort on one's part; it does not occur automatically. It must be initiated and maintained – it must be self-directed.

Prudence and self-direction are but two aspects of the same act, and though the conclusions of practical reason can be shared, the act of reasoning that constitutes the core of self-direction cannot. Thus it is through self-direction, the exercise of practical reason, that an excellence becomes an excellence for the individual, a constituent of *that* individual's flourishing. It is through self-directedness that individualization itself occurs and an 'abstract' excellence becomes concrete. Self-direction does not, then, make excellences more excellent or valuable; rather it is that excellences are inherently self-directed or chosen.

Despite Gray's insistence that there are versions of human flourishing, when he talks of excellences apart from self-direction, he treats them as if they were concretely the same for everyone and the individual brought nothing to their realization and value. This is, however, false. Interestingly enough, to speak of excellences apart from self-direction also leaves in doubt what it means to speak of versions of *human* flourishing, and this brings us to our second point. What, if anything, makes the excellences listed in the previous paragraphs *human* excellences? They are diverse and can be part of forms of life that are radically different, as Gray so frequently observes, but why are these excellences called 'human'? Or, more to our point, since the set of excellences that are deemed 'human' is not infinite, is there any basis for our decision to include or exclude an excellence?

This is a large and deep issue touching on such questions as whether there are defensible versions of essentialism, what it means exactly to speak of 'family resemblances', and whether it is indeed necessary that we have a basis for such decisions.[38] But it hardly seems that Gray believes there to be no basis for such a decision, given his statement that there is a generic character to the nature of human beings in virtue of which they are called 'human'. It would seem that we can at least say what it takes for an excellence to be *excluded* from the set of human excellences, and the most plausible basis for suggesting an act be excluded is that it involves no act of reason, no self-direction. The medieval monk must at least *realize* the value of his constrained existence for it to qualify as flourishing. It seems to us, then, quite incoherent to talk of *human* excellences apart from some measure of self-direction or choice.

Finally, pointing to examples of people who flourish in societies that do not provide principled protection of their liberty does not show that self-direction is not an essential ingredient to every form of human flourishing. Nor does it show that the value of self-direction can only be determined by an examination of the particular form of life to which people in these societies and cultures belong. In such societies as medieval Christendom or feudal Japan in the Edo period or, indeed, the Gulag of the Soviet Union, there can be areas of life in which some are able to integrate their circumstances into a form of flourishing. But this may be more of an argument for the diversity of forms of flourishing than it is for the absence of self-direction.

The issue, in any case, ought to be the nature of human flourishing itself and not the many factors that may be necessary for the existence of human flourishing or how people in various and different situations might fashion self-perfecting lives. Could human flourishing be human flourishing if self-direction were impossible? We think not, but clearly appeal to empirical examples alone will not settle the issue.[39]

Gray claims that objective pluralism prevents any ethical theory, especially a self-perfectionist virtue ethics, from being sufficiently determinate to provide content to the right to liberty. Gray sees rights as intermediaries between claims about human interests that are vital to human flourishing and claims about what obligations are reasonable to impose on others in respect of these interests. However, since the different forms of flourishing give rise to different valuations or weightings of these human interests, there is no uniquely rational way to determine the meaning and scope of liberty and thus furnish a theoretical and jurisprudential limit on the political process. Hard cases regarding what constitutes restraint of liberty abound. They are the rule, not the exception; and it is only the political process itself that can determine the meaning, scope and, indeed, validity, of the right to liberty.

Gray is correct to hold that there is no overarching account of human flourishing, not even a generic account, that can serve as a standard by which various goods, virtues and excellences are given their appropriate combination, pattern or weighting. If rights are tied to these various combinations, patterns or weightings of basic goods or interests, there is no way in which the meaning, scope and validity of the right to liberty can be defended theoretically. It must be worked out in the concrete political process.

Gray is also correct to note that the scope and content of the concept of 'liberty' cannot be specified without making an ethical commitment. Liberty is not merely the absence of external impediment or the ability to do whatever one wants. When conceived in this amoral fashion, there is no way even to understand what it *means* to promote liberty. If our wants conflict, and if my wants are given legal protection and yours are thus constrained, then while it is the case that my liberty has been protected and your liberty denied, we still cannot say that liberty has been promoted. Liberty, so viewed, becomes meaningless as a political ideal.

Gray is wrong, however, to assume that there is nothing that can be used from an account of human flourishing to provide meaning, scope and validity to the right to liberty. We must recall here the essential steps of how a self-perfectionist virtue ethics provides a basis for this right. Given that there are diverse forms of human flourishing and that our need for sociality is profound and open-ended, we need a political standard that will allow interpersonal life in its widest sense to be possible, without at the same time requiring the sacrifice of the lives, time and resources of any person or group to others.

We need to find a feature of human flourishing in which each and every person in the concrete situation has a necessary stake and whose protection is consistent with the diverse forms of flourishing. This feature, as we have seen, is self-directedness. Self-direction is both common to all forms of human flourishing, regardless of the level of achievement or specificity, and peculiar to each. It can therefore, as we have also seen, provide the basis for rights.

Securing the possibility that people can be self-directed when they live among others requires that people not be allowed to use the times, resources and lives of others for purposes to which they have not consented. Since, as noted earlier, the single most common and threatening encroachment upon self-directedness is the initiation of physical force by one person (or group) against another, rights of equal liberty – where no one is allowed to take action towards another that threatens or destroys the other's self-directedness – are what is politically required. We do not need, however, to reprise our earlier argument for the right to liberty here; our aim is simply to show that there is indeed something that an account of human flourishing can provide to give meaning, scope and validity to the right to liberty.

It should be noted, however, that Gray's failure to see that self-direction is central and necessary to the very nature of human flourishing is not the only source of his pessimism about sustaining an argument for the universal value of liberty. There is also his conception of political philosophy. Once again his acceptance of the Enlightenment's view of reasoning is evident, but this time it has to do with political philosophy.

It seems that Gray believes that there are no universal principles or theoretical limits on the political process because he accepts the idea that political philosophy is simply ethics writ large. For him the essence of the political problem is how to assist everyone in achieving their moral perfection or good. If this were truly the nature of politics, then Gray would be correct to claim that there can be no universal principles or theoretical limits on the political process, because there are, indeed, numerous versions of human flourishing and no way to base a universal principle on such versions without favouring one over the other.

However, it is not necessary to make the achievement of human flourishing the positive and direct aim of politics. It is precisely because there is such pluralism that there is a need for a type of principle that is concerned not with everyone achieving their moral good or self-perfection, but with the protection of that in which everyone has a necessary stake and whose protection will in principle not favour any version of human flourishing over any other. There is a need for a type of principle that will help make the pursuit of moral excellence by oneself and others morally compossible. This type of principle provides the basis for the political and legal protection of self-direction. This type of principle is what we have called a 'metanormative' principle.

The right to liberty is such a principle. Protecting this condition for the possibility of human flourishing – self-direction – can thus be the universal aim of politics.

There is a need to distinguish politics from normative ethics and to acknowledge that the basic principles of political philosophy, especially rights, are 'metanormative' principles. Further, there is a need to recognize that the function of the right to liberty is to establish, to interpret and to evaluate political/legal contexts so that the self-directedness of individuals is protected and the liberty under which they can achieve their self-perfection is secured.

The right to liberty does not provide people with guidance regarding how they ought to conduct themselves. It is not a claim about what is good for persons or an assertion of what obligations people owe each other. Nor is it an intermediary principle that expresses a reasonable compromise between these claims. The right to liberty does not aim at assisting people in achieving their self-perfection or, indeed, in protecting the existence of the numerous and various conditions that are necessary for people to self-perfect. The aim of the right to liberty is restricted to protecting only that condition for the achievement of human flourishing that everyone in the concrete situation has a necessary stake in, and whose protection does not in principle favour one version of self-perfection over another – namely, as said earlier, the political and legal protection of self-direction.

It should, therefore, be clear that it is possible for there to be versions of human flourishing that may be largely precluded in certain societies based on the right to liberty. There is no guarantee that all the conditions necessary for achieving the proper fit between generic goods, virtues and excellences and someone's nexus will be achieved or that the maintenance of social structures necessary for a form of flourishing to exist can be maintained. A political system based on the right to liberty does not dictate or guarantee what versions of human flourishing will exist or what the overall character of a society's culture will be.

There might be developments in societies that allow for the maximum compossible and equal freedom for everyone, yet tend to work against certain versions of human flourishing. We will discuss this issue in greater detail when we consider MacIntyre's objections to liberalism in the next section, but two points can be reiterated here. First, what versions of flourishing will advance or decline cannot be determined *a priori*, and this is not, in any case, the purpose of liberal politics. It is only a political hubris born of ethical rationalism that would allow political theorists to assume that they can so manage or control society that they can determine what versions of self-perfection or forms of life and culture will advance or decline. Second, no version of human flourishing is *as a matter of principle* ruled out by a political/jurisprudential system based on the right to liberty. There is no political attempt to make any version of human flourishing impossible.[40] It is therefore crucial to grasp that liberalism is a political philosophy, not an ethics. It does not try, with the right to liberty, to make it possible that everyone can flourish. To the extent that liberal theorists do in fact fail to grasp this point, Gray's criticisms of liberalism are devastating.

THE CHALLENGE OF CONSERVATIVE COMMUNITARIANISM

Liberalism in the name of freedom imposes a certain kind of unacknowledged domination, and one which in the long run tends to dissolve traditional human ties and to impoverish social and cultural relationships. Liberalism, while imposing through state power regimes that declare everyone free to pursue whatever they take to be their own good, deprives most people of the possibility of understanding their lives as a quest for the discovery and achievement of the good, especially by the way in which it attempts to discredit those traditional forms of human community within which this project has to be embodied.

Alasdair MacIntyre in *The American Philosopher*

John Gray's form of communitarianism still retains much sympathy with many of the components of liberalism. If nothing else, the irreconcilable plurality of goods makes it unlikely that Gray would favour an order that promoted a certain conception of the good or even the pursuit of goodness itself. In this respect, Gray could be considered a liberal communitarian.[41] Communitarianism, however, has more adherents to its conservative than its liberal wing. With few exceptions, perhaps no theorist is more associated with communitarianism than is Alasdair MacIntyre.[42] His form of communitarianism is one in which there is an unabashed belief in the role of politics in the promotion of virtue. It differs from ordinary forms of contemporary conservatism in its antipathy to anything tied to liberalism, such as markets or individual rights. In this respect, MacIntyre's communitarianism,[43] while somewhat more reactionary, is also amenable to those whose sympathies have always been towards the Left. Indeed, as MacIntyre has recently remarked in an interview, 'the Marxist's understanding of liberalism as ideological, as a deceiving and self-deceiving mask for certain social interests, remains compelling' (see Borradori 1994, 143).

Although liberalism has always had its critics, the communitarian critique led by MacIntyre has a particular importance to us, because MacIntyre claims that his position operates from an Aristotelian perspective. The suggestion is not only that an Aristotelian framework can be used to support the sort of communitarianism that MacIntyre advances but, more importantly, that it cannot be used to support liberalism. Obviously our remarks to this point can be taken as refuting the claim about the incompatibility of Aristotelianism and liberalism, but spending some time looking at the arguments made directly against liberalism should also help clarify both the nature of liberalism and our justification of it.

MacIntyre has many complaints regarding liberalism, including that it is connected to emotivism, subjectivism, relativism and atomism (MacIntyre 1981, Chapters 2–7, 17). Further, he complains about the primacy of rights in much liberal theory, which he regards as but another futile attempt to give priority to the right over the good in ethics. Nearly all of these complaints, however, have to do with ethical and anthropological views to which liberal political theory has traditionally been linked. This leaves open the possibility that liberal political theory might be linked to an ethical theory and view of human nature that are not so connected. Certainly the self-perfectionist virtue-ethics that has been presented in this essay is not guilty of emotivism, subjectivism, relativism, atomism or of giving the right priority over the good. Yet since we do endorse a notion of rights, we will concentrate on MacIntyre's basic objection to rights as primary political principles.

MacIntyre has two basic objections to liberalism's advocacy of the primacy of rights. The first complaint is philosophical, and the second is cultural and sociological. The philosophical complaint has three aspects: (1) rights are dependent on deeper ethical concepts and are thus not ethically primary (MacIntyre 1981, Chapters 6 and 9), and thus, (2) to handle adequately the complexities of moral life, finer conceptual tools than rights are required. Rights have too much of an all-or-nothing character to be of very much use in dealing with moral subtleties and are thus not sufficiently precise; (3) a political regime based on the right to liberty is actually inimical to the self-perfection of most people, because it destroys the various traditional forms of community life in which people's pursuit of their good is embodied (MacIntyre 1988, 335–45).

The cultural/sociological complaint, which MacIntyre shares with Charles Taylor (1985, 1989, 1991), holds that liberalism and liberal regimes cannot make rights ultimate or primary and maintain themselves for long. The very things that have made liberal civilization possible – the intellectual, cultural, scientific and moral prerequisites – cannot be maintained if the regime's ultimate moral message is simply liberty. More is necessary (MacIntyre 1981, Chapter 9).

Indeed there are already signs of the demise of liberal orders. The current inflation of rights claims – that is, the tendency to think that everything one needs, or even wants, somehow creates a right – is cutting great swaths through conventional forms of life and impoverishing the taxpayer. Further, even if one sharply distinguishes negative from positive rights, it still seems that the liberal society, especially today's United States, is losing the traditions and institutions that ultimately keep societies alive and functioning. Rights-talk has so invaded our ethical discourse and lives that we immediately turn to lawyers at the first sign of conflict. Morals, manners and other civilities that cannot be captured in such talk seem to have no role to play.

Given the character of the argument that has been advanced in this essay, it should not be surprising to learn that there is sympathy for some of these objections. They contain, however, both a fundamental confusion regarding rights and an overstatement of the role of social traditions in discovering and achieving the good. There is also an even deeper issue of how one understands human nature, which cannot be adequately dealt with here, but which nonetheless deserves comment.

As should be clear by now, rights are metanormative principles. Correctly understood, they provide the answer to liberalism's problem of how to find a standard that will allow interpersonal life in its widest sense to be possible, without at the same time requiring the sacrifice of the lives, time and resources of any persons or groups to others. Since sociality is not an option but a requirement for moral maturation, seeking a life of isolation, where one's self-direction could never be threatened by others, is not morally viable.

Thus it should be clear that the right to liberty is necessary to the possibility of self-perfection. However, it should also be clear that such a right deals with but one of the problems that human beings face in trying to find moral fulfilment – a crucial problem, one that is impossible to ignore, but still only one of the problems we face. Therefore, it should not be surprising to note that other moral concepts are needed to guide one towards human flourishing, and that the right to liberty provides little assistance in the task of directly and positively securing self-perfection. As noted earlier, even though all moral principles are based on human flourishing, this does not mean that they are reducible to the same logical type.

MacIntyre's philosophical complaint about liberalism's advocacy of the primacy of rights fails to consider that rights need to be the ultimate ethical concept only in regard to creating, interpreting and evaluating political/legal contexts in which normative activities can occur. Rights do not replace the virtues, including interpersonal ones such as charity and justice (see Den Uyl 1993, ch. 4; Den Uyl and Rasmussen in Machan and Rasmussen 1995); nor can they replace the role of manners and etiquette in social life. Rights cannot replace all the other necessary moral activities that are needed to make human living more than mere survival. Liberalism has not, however, always been clear on the role or function of rights, so this complaint by communitarianism is not without some justification. Yet once the metanormative character of rights is appreciated, the first two aspects of the philosophical complaint lose their force.

The third aspect of MacIntyre's philosophical complaint is very serious. Its basic thrust is that the liberal regime, by enforcing the basic right to liberty, destroys traditional forms of community life that embody people's efforts to pursue their flourishing. A liberal regime acts as a detriment to the lives of people by allowing their basic institutions to be destroyed. Liberalism does this by instrumentalizing everything, including its own institutions and principles. To survive, a society must see some goods as being internal to practices and not as objects to be manipulated in the service of some individual or group interest. Liberal politics thus centres around serving interests or resolving conflicts rather than being a practice which secures some good by its very engagement.

There is a difference, of course, between what a liberal regime allows and what it encourages or discourages. It is most certainly true that a liberal regime, by enforcing the right to liberty, allows people to decide for themselves whether they want to continue following traditional forms of community life or to try other new forms. There is, however, no principled commitment either to discourage traditional forms of community life or to encourage new forms. Therefore, it is hard to see how a liberal regime of the kind we have been defending throughout this essay could sensibly be accused of destroying traditional forms of community life.

It might be argued, however, that by allowing people to decide for themselves what forms of community life to pursue, the liberal regime in effect discredits the traditional forms of community life because it permits alternative forms to compete with them. Two points should be made here:

1. Allowing alternative forms of community life to compete with more traditional forms does not, in and of itself, mean or imply that the alternative forms of community life are as good for persons as the more traditional ones. To protect people's liberty to choose what form of community life they will adopt does not imply that any choice they make is as good as the next. It is only by confusing a metanormative principle with a normative principle that such a claim could be plausibly made.

2. The need for community life is not something abstract or impersonal. It is, like all the other goods that make up human flourishing, an individualized and agent-relative good. Thus it is not possible to know from our armchair whether a traditional form of community life is better for a person than an alternative one.

Indeed, MacIntyre (1981, 178, 204) makes the mistake of supposing that conformity to practices productive of goods internal to the practices themselves (as making book is internal to bridge) is the same as the production of a good. This is either gross conventionalism or false; for either one defines the goods in terms of such conformity (conventionalism) or one leaves open the question of whether that conformity is good. In the Aristotelian tradition, moral goodness is never determined by convention alone. Liberalism agrees. It would seem, then, that the feature of natural-rights classical liberalism with which MacIntyre might be taking ultimate issue is its naturalism (Rasmussen and Den Uyl 1991, 101).[44]

Wisdom might suggest that one should only with great care and consideration reject a traditional form of community life for some alternative, but it is certainly possible that such a rejection could be morally appropriate for a person. If the aim is for individuals to find community life that truly supports them in creating and fashioning worthwhile lives, it is important that they be allowed to use their practical reason as best they can in deciding what form of community life to adopt.

MacIntyre would seemingly reply, however, that these two responses assume that people can make judgements about what form of community life is best for them without also considering the crucial role played by their community's traditions and practices in their very understanding of who they are and what their lives are for. This is never the case. People's understanding of what is best for them is always learned through, and embodied in, the customs, traditions, culture and history of their community. Human moral judgements do not function autonomously, apart from the traditions and social structures in which human beings live. Thus there is no way that people can try to distance themselves from their influence. There simply is no abstract understanding of what is good for human beings over and above what is embodied in human communities. As MacIntyre (1981, 204–5) observes:

> For I am never able to seek for the good or exercise the virtues only *qua* individual. This is partly because what it is to live the good life concretely varies from circumstance to circumstance even when it one of the same conception of the good life and one and the same set of virtues which are being embodied in a human life. What the good life is for a fifth-century Athenian general will not be the same as what it was for a medieval nun or a seventeenth-century farmer. But it is not just that different individuals live in different social circumstances; it is also that we all approach our own circumstances as bearers of a particular social identity. I am someone's son or daughter, someone else's cousin or uncle; I am a citizen of this or that city, a member of this or that guild or profession; I belong to this clan, that tribe, this nation. What is good for me has to be good for one who inhabits these roles. As such, I inherit from the past of my family, my city, my tribe, my nation, a variety of debts, inheritances, rightful expectations and obligations. These constitute the given of my life, my moral starting point. This is in part what gives my life moral particularity.

By allowing people the liberty to question the very workings of their community, the liberal regime destroys the only basis people have for discovering and achieving their good.

Our short response[45] is simply that, in order to evaluate how well a person's community promotes one's human flourishing, it is not necessary to deny that people's understanding of who they are, what their lives are for, and thus what is good for them is influenced greatly by their community's traditions and practices. To admit this, however, does not rule out the possibility that some aspects of what one has learned may be false and that one can determine what these aspects are. Though highly unlikely, it is even possible that one's community may have gotten things entirely wrong.

Furthermore, one can have an abstract understanding of human flourishing that is not contentless. As we have noted many times, the virtues and goods that constitute human flourishing exist only in an individualized manner; nonetheless, it is true that we can, through abstraction, apprehend the constituents of human flourishing just as such. We can talk of the virtues and generic goods of human flourishing and thus have knowledge that, though it may be incomplete and reflect cultural influences, is sufficient for us to evaluate what we have received from our community.

Though human flourishing must always be embodied in some form of community life, it is not necessarily limited to the ones with which a person is acquainted. Nor is human flourishing defined merely by the customs and practices of one's community. MacIntyre comes dangerously close to assuming that the customary morality of a particular society, *Sittlichkeit*, and impersonal moral theory, *Moralität*, exhaust all the possible conceptions of morality (see MacIntyre 1994b). Yet we have seen in this essay an outline of a self-perfectionist virtue ethics that is neither. A virtue ethics is not simply customary morality.[46]

It would seem, however, that an issue of sociological reductionism is being raised: does human sociality exhaustively account for, at the most basic level, what it is to be human? Though we are certainly not Cartesian egos or Kantian noumenal selves that operate in isolation, apart from natural and social reality, are we to assume that who and what we are (or what our good consists in) is something entirely and solely determined by our social relations? Is our capacity to reason, engage in abstract considerations of the nature of things, make moral judgements and conduct ourselves accordingly something that is entirely and solely determined by the traditions and practices of our community? Or are there not features of who and what each of us is that exist, and are what they are, whether the traditions and practices of our community recognize them or not? MacIntyre cannot allow his position to reduce to a conventionalism and thus a form of ethical non-cognitivism. If this were so, then one of his basic reasons for rejecting liberalism – that it is based on ethical non-cognitivism – would be disarmed.

The temptation in MacIntyre's thought to view 'nature' and 'nurture' as mutually exclusive alternatives, which any view of human nature or human flourishing must choose between, and to adopt sociological reductionism is most revealing. It shows a failure to distinguish between: (1) thinking of human nature or human flourishing without thinking about their social and cultural embodiment, and (2) thinking that human nature or human flourishing does not have a social and cultural embodiment. The first of these does not involve a falsehood and the second does. But there is no good reason to suppose that an abstract consideration of human nature or human flourishing requires doing (2).

Just as the abstraction 'length' does not exclude quantity but simply does not specify the amount, so the abstractions 'human nature' or 'human flourishing' do not exclude the social or cultural form in which they may exist, but simply do not specify what determination they may take. We cannot, however, enter into a discussion of the nature of abstraction here, but it is nonetheless important to note that MacIntyre seems to adopt a view of abstraction that is typically modern, for it supposes that the process of abstraction necessarily leaves out or excludes aspects of something's nature and thus can only provide a partial comprehension.[47] This supposition is in fundamental opposition to that espoused by Aquinas, who argues that abstraction does not necessarily exclude or leave out aspects of something's nature (Aquinas 1968, 37–44). It is ironic, to say the least, that MacIntyre, who claims superiority for the Thomistic tradition of inquiry (1988, 402–3), should avail himself of one of more problematic epistemological tenets of modernity and ignore the Thomistic approach to abstraction.

Our main point here is simply this: human nature, including the human good, must have some particular cultural and social manifestation but, abstractly considered, it can have virtually any.[48] Thus the particular cultural and social manifestation of human nature or the human good should never be taken as defining or constituting human nature or the human good itself.[49] Liberalism is the only political form that recognizes this truth.

It might, however, be replied that all this still misses the point that MacIntyre and other communitarians[50] are making. Granted that the liberal regime does not require the destruction of traditional forms of community life, is this not what generally happens in a liberal regime? Is this not what life in a liberal regime is actually like? In the real world, are not people in general so dominated by liberalism's emphasis on liberty that the institutions through which they endeavour to discover and achieve their moral well-being are destroyed?

These questions cannot be answered here, for they involve more than philosophical considerations. Historical, cultural and sociological studies are needed. Yet if this is the level of inquiry at which communitarianism's concerns about liberalism are to be discussed, then there are questions that need to be asked about communitarian social orders.

Assuming that we can get a clear understanding of what is meant by 'community', what is real life in such social orders generally like? Are they really orders where everyone works in solidarity for a single common end, or do they tend to destroy all chances people have to flourish in their unique and diverse ways? How is the individualized and agent-relative character of human flourishing handled, or is it just denied or ignored? Are some persons always and necessarily sacrificed for the common good of the community? In what manner, if any, is the open-ended character of human sociality allowed to exist? Is there any evidence that diversity is a central feature of non-liberal orders? Can one conceptually reject liberalism's openness and plausibly embrace diversity? Can people choose to adopt a way of life with others that conflicts with the values of the community? How are conflicts between different forms of community life met? Are there different forms? It is, to say the least, not obvious that the real, everyday lives of most people in a communitarian political order are better than those in a liberal one.

We are brought, then, to the cultural/sociological complaint – namely that liberal regimes cannot make rights ultimate or primary and maintain themselves for long. This complaint has merit. A liberal regime cannot long maintain itself if the only ethical message found in the society and culture that it protects is simply the right to liberty. Indeed many things need to be done for liberal regimes to flourish; but first liberalism needs to be clear about the function of the political/legal order.

In the version of liberalism that we have been defending, this function has been made clear; but this has not generally been the case. Insofar as liberal theorists have not clearly recognized the difference between normative and metanormative principles, and insofar as they have thought that liberalism's political principles could be maintained without a deeper ethical commitment, theorists of liberalism have helped to create the very forces that are leading to its demise.

Furthermore, the tendency in American liberalism to make a right out of every need (sometimes even a want) has made the concept of rights nearly otiose. Instead of rights being confined to issues about the basic conditions of a political/legal order, they have been used to replace crucial moral concepts, such as the virtues, which are primarily concerned with people achieving worthwhile moral lives. This has confused and damaged both forms of ethical language. In fact, to some people, it appears that the right to liberty is nothing more than a licence to do whatever one wants, and that to call something a moral virtue is to demand a law compelling universal compliance with it. *The ethical language of liberalism in the United States has been virtually deconstructed!*

The solution to this problem is, however, not to deny the importance of rights-talk as something distinct from other ethical language. Rather it is to understand clearly the rationale for liberal political institutions being concerned only with the right to liberty. It has been the aim of this essay to provide such a rationale and thus defend liberalism. It should be recalled, in this connection, that the point of that rationale was to show that the very sociality of human flourishing, together with its individualized and agent-relative character, creates a profound need for a special kind of ethical language.

When it comes to creating, interpreting and evaluating political/legal orders, an ethical language is needed – not for the purpose of providing guidance to people in finding moral fulfilment – but rather for the purpose of providing a context in which all the diverse forms of human flourishing may exist together in an ethically compossible manner. The ethical language for this task is the language of metanormativity, as opposed to normativity. *The natural right to liberty is the basic metanormative principle.*

Not only is there an ethical justification for the liberal regime, but also, *qua* political institution, liberalism does not extend its ethical message beyond respect for the basic right to liberty. It is morally necessary that there be a political theory that argues that not everything is or should be political, and this limitation on political action even applies to many of the activities that are socially and culturally necessary for the maintenance of liberal regimes. MacIntyre often begs the question by assuming that the purpose of politics is to promote an ethical vision of some sort – a role he may wish to assign to politics, but one liberalism rejects.

In the end, however, there is no substitute for the need to care about the moral life, the role of virtue and the importance of personal responsibility. People need to care about the ethical justifications of their social and political institutions. They need to understand better the nature of the arguments that can be used to defend the liberal regime. Further, they need to create institutions and traditions that explain and illustrate the importance of a political/legal system's being based on the right to liberty. These are very important matters to which the role of intellectuals is not insignificant.

5. Conclusion

We have sought to defend liberalism by linking modern politics with a pre-modern moral tradition. As we noted in the introduction, this combination is itself a kind of post-modernism. The reason for this claim can now be readily seen. We embrace many views that are frequently thought to work against modern political theory. For example, we hold the following: that human beings are naturally social; that ethical subjectivism is not an adequate moral theory; that a virtue ethics more successfully captures the nature of the moral life than any other; that practical reasoning is not merely instrumental reasoning and is crucial for ethics; that ethical rationalism is false because it fails to recognize the role of the particular and contingent in determining proper conduct and thus how pluralistic the human good truly is; that impersonal moral theory with its use of the universalizability principle is an inadequate and distorting way either to criticize the status quo or defend liberalism; that liberty cannot be defined or understood without an ethical commitment; that any theory of rights which is capable of motivating human conduct must ultimately be based on a view of the human good; and that rights are not ethically fundamental or sufficient to maintain a liberal order.

We have, however, shown that these claims, despite their pre-modern or even 'communitarian' character do not lead to the usual identification of politics with ethics, either in the moral sense of viewing politics as simply ethics writ large, or in the managerial sense that sees ethics as primarily concerned with the establishment and maintenance of a certain form of social order. No, it is in securing some of the necessary *conditions* for undertaking action among others in pursuit of a moral and flourishing life that constitutes the proper province of politics, and the point at which politics and ethics interface.

Contrary to the tendencies of modern philosophy, these conditions are based on an understanding of the human good, specifically, a neo-Aristotelian understanding of human flourishing, and thus they have a moral foundation. Appealing to such a view of the human good does not, however, make the connection between politics and ethics either direct or isomorphic. As we observed in the penultimate paragraph of the final chapter of *Liberty and Nature*:

> The paradigm of the two basic world views (modern and classical) we have presented is not so rigid as we have made it seem. Liberalism actually leaves the possibility of moral perfection open. All it says is that we must first solve the problem of social conflict before we can worry about perfection. And antiquity is not necessarily opposed to the idea that perfection must be achieved in stages and that such stages may involve certain preconditions that must be met and maintained if further advancement is to be achieved. Furthermore, antiquity is not necessarily committed to the notion that the state must be the vehicle by which people are directed to their proper ends. The logical openings in both traditions make our position possible. What we have done is to take advantage of them and to indicate a possible means of reconciling morality and liberty (Rasmussen and Den Uyl 1991, 224–5).

The openness of liberalism to an ethics of self-perfection and the idea that self-perfection must be achieved in stages led us in our earlier work, and even more so in this one, to see that the key to understanding and defending liberalism is found in the language of metanormativity. The basis for this understanding and defence is the realization that though the value of self-direction is of comparatively little importance in ethics, it is of supreme importance when it comes to determining what the conditions for civil order should be and thus what the proper function of natural rights is. To find something that will allow social life in its widest sense to be possible, despite all the varieties of human flourishing, and yet not require the lives and resources of some to be at the service of others, is the aim of rights and remains the principal reason why liberalism so understood is a precondition for civilized social life and the pursuit of self-perfection.

Notes

1. Spinoza, for example, is explicit about this: '[Philosophers] conceive men, not as they are, but as they would like them to be. The result is that they have generally written satire instead of ethics, and have never conceived a political system which can be applied in practice; but have produced either obvious fantasies, or schemes that could only have been put into effect in Utopia, or the poets golden age, where, of course, there was no need of them at all' *(Tractatus Politicus* I, 1).

2. This is also what we believe Spinoza was after, despite the use of the term 'ethics' in the passage cited in note 1. That is, Spinoza wanted to replace what we might call 'normative political theory' with social science.

3. The distinction really owes its origins to John Rawls (see 1971). We are uncertain how much support for it can be given using the classical writings of liberalism (for example, Locke, Hume, Constant, and so on), but the distinction has become such a part of the contemporary literature that we feel justified in treating it as a central conceptual distinction of liberalism. Rawls himself now feels the pain of trying to separate the right and the good too much (see Rawls, 1993, Lecture V). This rather confirms our point of liberalism's continual vacillation between the two.

4. Some recent liberal theories have foregone this option by making the good agent-relative but not the right (see, for example, Mack (1995)). This differs from the traditional approach because the agent-relativity of the good is given moral status, thus creating a moral dualism. Our view of this position is that it is as unstable as its traditional counterparts and that the endeavour to reconcile the good and the right is an awareness of the potential tension between them. Of course one can clearly subordinate the one to the other, but this is just another way of saying that liberalism is grounded in the right but not the good.

5. It is not clear why, if we remove (or add, depending on the perspective) all the constraints we would not simply end up with the world we have already. For if we suppose all agents to be rational and bargaining to their best advantage under any given set of conditions and with the information they have, then the outcome should be rational as well and constitute an accurate description of the world as it actually exists.

6. It is tempting to say that if we just distinguish between moral and non-moral goods we can reconcile the low good, the high good and the right into one theory. But the idea that there is super- and sub-erogation is itself a function of the distinction between the good and the right and the final irrelevance of the good to a determination of the right. There is less a reconciliation than a rejection here.

7. A contemporary example of this might be Alan Gewirth, who wishes us to see our own good in terms of the freedom and well-being we imply in our actions towards others (see Gewirth 1978). As we note below, this procedure does not seem limited to just deontic theories. Mill seems to recommend identifying one's good with the well-being of society, although it may be this very concept of 'well-being' that is to mark the difference. For the idea that utilitarianism is really a kind of deontologism, see Henry B. Veatch, 1971, 152. The most common tendency in

equating the good with the right is to reduce all of ethics to issues of justice (see Den Uyl, 1993).

8. An example of its depth comes with respect to the uses of knowledge in society. See Thomas Sowell (1980, Chapter 1).

9. In this respect our views are similar to those of Rawls's, who argues that the priority of the right over the good is central to liberalism and a good thing. As an example of how true this is at the deepest level, Will Kymlicka (1989), in arguing against Rawls, tries to suggest that there is no real issue about the priority of the right and the good (p. 21). Rawls has misconceived utilitarianism. 'It is the concern with equal consideration that underlies the arguments of Bentham and Sidgwick ... and is explicitly affirmed by recent utilitarians ... (p. 25). Of course, to underlie a doctrine with 'equal consideration' is just to give priority to the right over the good at the deepest level.

10. We use the term 'separating' rather than 'distinguishing' deliberately here, for part of our point is that what began as simply a distinction becomes a separation as time moves on.

11. Our point is, of course, not that every liberal doctrine is really a deontology in disguise, but that the tendency is in that direction.

12. To reject an identification of liberalism with ethics is not to reject a connection between the two. An examination of the nature of the connection is found in our discussion of metanormative principles and rights.

13. The new liberalism was actually an effort to bring some content back into ethics (or ethics back into liberalism). Its main problem is doing so and still qualifying as a liberalism.

14. A term given to liberals in the 19th century who sought more state intervention in social life and who tended to hold a more robust conception of the ethical good than their classical counterparts.

15. The process, we believe, began much earlier with the increasing political control and influence of the Church. Since religion speaks predominantly in normative terms, its connection to political life would necessarily begin to see the ethical in terms of the social rather than primarily in terms of personal salvation. The rejection of the Catholic Church during the Reformation was not a rejection of this feature of the relationship between ethics and politics as Calvin's *Geneva* indicates.

16. Alasdair MacIntyre, for example, speaks of the 'privatization' of the good (MacIntyre 1994a, 1–17).

17. For an indication that this was once not the case, see Den Uyl (1993).

18. We, of course, argue that nothing could be further from the truth than to saying that liberalism and Aristotelianism are opposed. We would agree with MacIntyre, however, to the extent that the 'opposition' would be greater without the metanormative distinction.

19. It would be a mistake to interpret our remarks here as implying that liberalism was previously oblivious to our point here. In fact, Spinoza in Chapters XIV–XX of the *Tractatus Theologico-Politicus* indicates the distinction between the norms provided by the state and ethical salvation or blessedness. Adam Smith (*The Theory of Moral Sentiments*, VI. ii. Introduction) distinguishes ethics from jurisprudence as being two separate parts of 'moral philosophy'. Moreover, in the early American experience it was not uncommon to speak of rights as a 'power...to act in a moral way', suggesting a distinction between moral action *per se* and rights, although the exact role of morality here was confused (see James H. Hutson (1994)).

20. Perhaps Kant comes close with his distinction between the categorical imperative and all other rules.

21. In saying this we are clearly rejecting the view that sees liberalism as abstract

universal rules plus personal interests, such that one is either referring to one or the other. In our schema there are liberal norms, ethical norms and personal interests.

22. The metaethical presuppositions of the ethics we believe most in accord with liberalism's nature should be made clear in the next section and following.

23. Some values – perhaps 'fairness' is – might be interpreted in ways that are metanormative and ways that are straightforwardly moral. This problem only adds to the confusion of which we speak.

24. The section on ethics to follow and the one on rights should indicate how it avoids these problems.

25. A number of liberal authors come close to this. For example, Hayek speaks of 'purpose-independent' rules which do not aim at the promotion of any one value (Hayek 1973, 112–14). However, while authors sometimes recognize different levels of rules, they fail to understand the relationship between the rules and morality, and so they either succumb to the temptation to regard the general abstract rules as moral rules or they diminish the substantive character of morality by reducing it to conflict avoidance or rights-respecting conduct.

26. John Gray is fond of citing Joseph Raz's contention that rights are not primitive but based in the end on interests (Gray 1995, 119). The interests we develop, however, are just as dependent on the rights we possess. Little seems to be gained from this chicken/egg sort of dispute.

27. There are, of course, some who would urge that there are completed liberal individuals with their own 'liberal virtues' (see, for example, Macedo, 1990).

28. In *After Virtue*, MacIntyre (1981) argued for social teleology and dismissed the possibility of a naturalistic basis for natural ends. In a more recent work, MacIntyre (1992, 3–19) seems to suggest that a theistically grounded account of teleology is the best hope for the idea of natural ends. Yet see Rasmussen and Den Uyl (1991, 41–6) for a discussion of how teleology might be naturalistically grounded in a scientifically respectable way. See also Fred D. Miller, Jr (1995, 336-346) for a discussion of how natural teleology might be defended.

29. The weighting that is given by person A to his achievement of flourishing, Fa, is greater than that which A gives to B's achievement of flourishing, Fb. In other words, Fa gives A the primary moral responsibility of achieving Fa without implying any such responsibility to A for B achieving Fb, and vice versa.

30. The term 'volitional consciousness' is taken from Ayn Rand (Rand 1964, 20), but the concept is as old as Aristotle (see *De Anima*, II, 5). Further, it should be noted that 'self-direction' refers not merely to psychic events but to actions in space and time of flesh and blood human beings. It does not refer to the actions of some 'homunculus'.

31. Fred D. Miller, Jr (1995) points out that Aristotle had some conception of rights but that he was not a political liberal.

32. 'Maximum' here does not mean a utilitarianism of spheres of freedom where total freedom might be maximized by giving some people a larger sphere than others. The 'spheres' are a product, not a premise, of our theory.

33. See Rasmussen and Den Uyl (1991, 101–8) on the conditions that need to be fulfilled if rights are to be irreducible moral concepts.

34. This is, of course, the essence of Rousseau's critique in *Contrat Social* of Hobbes's discussion of the state of nature. We, however, reverse the point here to some extent. Rousseau says that Hobbes's state of nature is full of civilized men. We are saying that the moral revulsion at natural rights violations imports ideas of proper treatment in a civilized setting.

35. Indeed, Hobbes's mixture of metanormative with normative rules is perhaps the historical culprit here.

36. Gray is approvingly quoting Isaiah Berlin (1991, 80).
37. To better appreciate our approach to these matters, we should explain our understanding of the generic characteristics of our nature. We understand them, 'as a package of capacities whose realization is required for self-perfection, but whose form is individuated by each person's own attributes, circumstances, and interests. These generic capacities, then, constitute the skeletal structure of one's life, but do not provide that life with specific content or direction. It is precisely the genericism of these capacities that often renders them impotent as specific guides of conduct or character development; for, although grounded in reality, they are nevertheless generalized abstractions of common needs and capacities and not independent realities in their own right. As such, unless the matter at hand concerns people in general, there is no reason to suppose identity of expression among individuals. Consequently, as components of a skeletal framework, these generic capacities serve to channel or corral individual expressions of self-actualization, but are not of themselves sufficient to identify the particular forms of that expression. And because of their generic quality, they are not in conflict, since they are not yet sufficiently substantive to identify a basis for conflict. Individuals or society may breathe content into these capacities in such a way that conflicts do develop' (Den Uyl, 1991, 167–8).
38. Beyond expressing some very general anti-foundationalist remarks and offering an endorsement of the primacy of practice in the constitution of knowledge, Gray offers little definition of, and no argument for, anti-foundationalism or the primacy of practice. Nor does he address these questions.
39. The history of philosophy bears witness to the over-employment by philosophers of conceptual methods and insights to solve issues that require empirical input, but it is also true that we have in this century suffered from the reverse error – namely refusing to see that conceptual methods and insights into the nature of something are a necessary part of an answer to almost any question. Thus we ask: if human beings were attached to machines that satisfied their every need and thus made it unnecessary for them to do anything, that is, if everything were done for them so that they were essentially passive, would their lives be worthwhile? The nature of human flourishing is such that the answer to this question is 'no'. There would be no self-direction, no reason and no individualization. In a profound way, no one's life would really be his. There would be no such thing as self-perfection or human flourishing.
40. There might, however, appear to be an exception to the last statement, because versions of human flourishing that require the coercive use of other people's lives, time and resources are legally banned. Indeed the murderer, rapist, thief, extortionist and defrauder cannot legally practise their activities, but these activities do not constitute a form of flourishing. These activities not only lack the generic character to qualify as versions of self-perfection, they conflict with the minimal requirements for someone perfecting their natural sociality. They put severe limits on one's social relations and result in cutting one off from most of society, especially when considered over a lifetime.
41. Robert Nozick has also modified his commitment to negative rights and libertarianism and embraced a communitarian perspective (see Nozick 1989, 286–7), so he might fall under this classification, but he has said very little in defence of his new position.
42. Despite his classification as such by commentators (see note 43), MacIntyre does not consider himself to be communitarian. In his reply to Philip Pettit in John Horton and Susan Mendus (eds) (1994, 302), he states that whenever he has had the opportunity he has strongly disassociated himself from contemporary communitarians. We believe, however, that Mulhall and Swift (1992, 93) have

determined why MacIntyre is best understood as a communitarian. They observe that for MacIntyre, 'the very possibility of sustaining rationality and objectivity in the arena of moral and political evaluation depends on locating individuals and their arguments with other individuals within an overarching and nested set of inherently social matrixes…[I]n MacIntyre's view, failing to recognize the way in which human beings can be and are constitutively attached to their communities entails an inability to give a coherent account of the circumstances necessary to achieve *any* kind of human good (whether communal in content or not), for in absence of such constitutive communal frame works, the very idea of morality as a rational or intelligible enterprise drops out.' We will see support for this observation in the discussion of MacIntyre's views that follows.

43. Alasdair MacIntyre's communitarian objections to liberalism may be found in his books: After *Virtue* (1981), *Whose Justice? Which Rationality?* (1988) and *Three Rival Versions of Moral Enquiry* (1990). Also, the following works have essays by MacIntyre or discuss his work: Markate Daly (ed.) (1994), Stephen Mulhall and Adam Swift (eds) (1992) and C.F. Delaney (ed.) (1994).

44. We cannot take up a discussion of ontological issues here. But if naturalism is rejected, if the nature of anything is totally explained by the traditions and practices of one's community, we cannot help but ask: how can MacIntyre complain that the notion of 'community' in liberal societies, infused with Enlightenment values, is somehow inadequate? To what can he appeal? Internal justification will not suffice, because people will adhere to these values despite inconsistencies, and they might ask why they should value consistency over their community's traditions and practices.

45. See T.H. Irwin (1989). This is a careful examination and critique of MacIntyre's view of rationality in *Whose Justice? Which Rationality?* (MacIntyre 1988).

46. See Fred D. Miller, Jr (1995). Miller shows Aristotle's self-perfectionist virtue ethics not to be confined to mere community standards and that his politics is open to natural rights.

47. Modern philosophers generally treat abstraction as a process of 'picking out' some feature and excluding others (see, for example, John Locke (1959, 83–4)). Accordingly, 'rational animal' means only some combination of rationality and animality, and 'social animal' means only some combination of sociality and animality, but they carry no further signification. Yet it is not necessary to accept such a view of abstraction (see Aquinas (1968) and note 48).

48. Abstraction need not be understood as excluding the differentiating traits of something's nature, but can be understood as a consideration of the whole nature of something that is done in a distinctive way – namely, the differentiating traits of something's nature are not expressed. When differentiating traits of a nature are not expressed, they are treated as implicit, and this means that the differentiating traits of a nature that is being considered are not specified. Yet this type of consideration does require that they exist in some determinate form but can – within a certain range – exist in any. For example, to consider a human being *as such* is not to specify the colour, size or shape, but it is necessary that a human being have some determinate colour, size or shape. The signification of a concept formed by such a process of abstraction is thus not confined to some part of a being's nature, but signifies that nature entirely. What is not expressed in abstraction may not, however, be discerned by simply a process of *inspectio mentis*. Rationalistic analysis will not work. There is a crucial role for sense-perception in human knowledge, as well as insight into the contingent and particulars in which a nature always and necessarily exists, but it is nonetheless possible for a concept to apprehend the whole nature of something, and not just a part (see Douglas B. Rasmussen (1994) for a discussion of this alternative view of abstraction). Thus an

abstract understanding of human beings, such as 'rational animal', can be formed without excluding any cultural or social conditions from such an understanding, and 'social animal' can be formed without excluding any natural capacities or individuating conditions.

49. However, MacIntyre (1981, 70) has stated that, 'there seems something deeply mistaken in the notion... that there are two distinct subjects or disciplines – moral philosophy, a set of conceptual inquiries, on the one hand, and the sociology of morals, a set of empirical hypotheses and findings, on the other. Quine's death-blow to any substantial version of the analytic-synthetic distinction casts doubt on this kind of contrast between the conceptual and the empirical'. Nonetheless, it does not follow from Quine's rejection of conceptual analysis of meanings that the notion of essence or nature is thereby rendered senseless. Conceptual pragmatism is not required; the door remains open to versions of essentialism (see Douglas B. Rasmussen (1984)). Thus the differences between subject matters or disciplines, for example, moral philosophy and the sociology of morals, could be based on something real.

50. Besides Charles Taylor (1985, 1989, 1991), Amitai Etzioni (1991, 1995) and Michael J. Sandel (1982) could be mentioned in this connection as well. For an important critique of MacIntyre and Sandel, see Jeffrey Paul and Fred D. Miller Jr (1990). Finally, see Chandran Kukathas (1996) for a criticism of the exaggerated value and centrality that both contemporary liberalism and communitarianism give political community.

Bibliography

Ackrill, J. (1973), *Aristotle's Ethics*, New York: Humanities Press.

Aquinas, T. (1968), *Being and Essence*, revised and translated by A. Maurer, Toronto: The Pontifical Institute of Mediaeval Studies.

Berlin, I. (1969), *Four Essays On Liberty*, New York: Oxford University Press.

Berlin, I. (1982), *Against the Current*, edited by H. Hardy, New York: Penguin Books.

Berlin, I. (1991), *The Crooked Timber of Humanity*, New York: Alfred A. Knopf.

Borradori, G. (1994), *The American Philosopher: Conversations with Quine, Davidson, Putnam, Nozick, Danto, Rorty, Cavell, MacIntyre, and Kuhn*, translated by Rosanna Crocitto, Chicago: University of Chicago Press.

Daly, M. (ed.) (1994), *Communitarianism: A New Public Ethics*, Belmont, California: Wadsworth Publishing.

Delaney, C. (ed.) (1994), *The Liberalism–Communitarian Debate*, Lanham, Maryland: Rowman & Littlefield.

Den Uyl, D.J. (1991), *The Virtue of Prudence*, New York: Peter Lang.

Den Uyl, D.J. (1993), 'The right to welfare and the virtue of charity', *Social Philosophy and Policy*, **10**, 192–224.

Den Uyl, D.J. and D.B. Rasmussen (1995), '"Rights" as metanormative principles', in T.R. Machan and D.B. Rasmussen (eds), *Liberty for the Twenty-First Century*, Lanham, Maryland: Rowman & Littlefield, pp. 59–75.

Etzioni, A. (1991), *The Spirit of Community*, New York: Crown Publishers.

Etzioni, A. (ed.) (1995), *Rights and the Common Good: The Communitarian Perspective*, New York: St Martin's Press.

George, R. (1993), *Making Men Moral*, Oxford: Clarendon Press.

Gewirth, A. (1978), *Reason and Morality*, Chicago: University of Chicago Press.

Gray, J. (1986), *Liberalism*, Milton Keynes and Minneapolis: Open University and Minnesota University Press.

Gray, J. (1989), *Liberalisms: Essays in Political Philosophy*, New York and London: Routledge.

Gray, J. (1993), *Post-Liberalism: Studies in Political Thought*, New York and London: Routledge.

Gray, J. (1994), 'After the new liberalism', *Social Research*, **61**, 719–35.

Gray, J. (1995), 'Agonistic liberalism', *Social Philosophy & Policy*, **12**, 111–35.

Gray, J. (1996), *Isaiah Berlin*, Princeton: Princeton University Press.

Guttman, A. (1985), 'Communitarian critics of liberalism', *Philosophy & Public Affairs*, **14**, 308–22.

Hayek, F. (1944), *The Road to Serfdom*, Chicago: Chicago University Press.

Hayek, F. (1973), *Rules and Order*, Vol. 1 of *Law, Legislation and Liberty*, Chicago: University of Chicago Press.

Horton, J. and S. Mendus (eds) (1994), *After MacIntyre*, Notre Dame, Indiana: Notre Dame University Press.

Hutson, J. (1994), 'The emergence of the modern concept of a right in America: the contribution of Michel Villey', *American Journal of Jurisprudence*, **39**, 185–224.

Irwin, T.H. (1989), 'Tradition and reason in the history of ethics', *Social Philosophy & Policy*, **7**, 45–68.

Kant, I. (1930), *Lecture on Ethics*, Indianapolis and Cambridge: Hackett Publishing Co.

Kukathas, C. (1990), *Hayek and Modern Liberalisms*, Oxford: Clarendon Press.

Kukathas, C. (1995), 'Freedom of association and liberty of conscience'. Paper presented at the American Political Science Association Convention 31 August–3 September, Chicago.

Kukathas, C. (1996), 'Liberalism, communitarianism, and political community', *Social Philosophy & Policy*, **13**, 80–104.

Kymlicka, W. (1989), *Liberalism, Community, and Culture*, Oxford: Clarendon Press.

Lerner, R. (1979), 'Commerce and character: the Anglo-American as new model man', *William and Mary Quarterly*, **36**, 3–26.

Locke, J. (1959), *An Essay Concerning Human Understanding*, A.C. Fraser (ed.), New York: Dover.

Lomasky, L.E. (1987), *Persons, Rights, and the Moral Community*, New York: Oxford University Press.

Lomasky, L.E. (1995), 'Liberal obituary?', in T.R. Machan and D.B.

Rasmussen (eds), *Liberty for the Twenty-First Century*, Lanham, Maryland: Rowman & Littlefield, pp. 243–58.

Lukes, S. (1994), 'The singular and plural: on the distinctive liberalism of Isaiah Berlin', *Social Research*, **61**, 687–717.

Lukes, S. (1995), 'Pluralism is not enough', *Times Literary Supplement*, 10 February, 4–5.

Macedo, S. (1990), *Liberal Virtues*, Oxford: Clarendon Press.

Machan, T.R. (1975), *Human Rights and Human Liberties*, Chicago: Nelson-Hall.

Machan, T.R. (1989), *Individuals and Their Rights*, LaSalle, Illinois: Open Court.

Machan, TR. and D.B. Rasmussen (eds) (1995), *Liberty for the Twenty-First Century*, Lanham, Maryland: Rowman & Littlefield.

MacIntyre, A. (1981), *After Virtue,* Notre Dame, Indiana: University of Notre Dame Press.

MacIntyre, A. (1988), *Whose Justice? Which Rationality?*, Notre Dame, Indiana: University of Notre Dame Press.

MacIntyre, A. (1990), *Three Rival Versions of Moral Enquiry*, Notre Dame, Indiana: Notre Dame University Press.

MacIntyre, A. (1992), 'Plain persons and moral philosophy: rules, virtues and goods', *American Catholic Philosophical Quarterly*, **66**, 3–19.

MacIntyre, A. (1994a), 'The privatization of the good: an inaugural lecture', in C.F. Delaney (ed.), *The Liberalism-Communitarianism Debate*, Lanham, Maryland: Rowman & Littlefield, pp. 1–17.

MacIntyre, A. (1994b), 'Is patriotism a virtue?', in M. Daly (ed.), *Communitarianism: A New Public Ethics*, Belmont, California: Wadsworth Publishing, pp. 307–18.

Mack, E. (1993a), 'Isaiah Berlin and the quest for liberal pluralism', *Public Affairs Quarterly*, **7**, 215–30.

Mack, E. (1993b), 'Personal integrity, practical recognition, and rights', *The Monist*, **76**, 101–18.

Mack, E. (1995), 'Moral individualism and libertarian theory', in T.R. Machan and D.B. Rasmussen (eds), *Liberty for the Twenty-First Century*, Lanham, Maryland: Rowman & Littlefield, pp. 41–58.

Miller Jr, F. (1995), *Nature, Justice, and Rights in Aristotle's* Politics, Oxford: Clarendon Press.

Mulhall, S. and A. Swift (eds) (1992), *Liberals & Communitarians*, Oxford: Blackwell.

Norton, D. (1976), *Personal Destinies*, Princeton: Princeton University Press.

Nozick, R. (1974), *Anarchy, State, and Utopia*, New York: Basic Books.

Nozick, R. (1989), *The Examined Life*, New York: Simon & Schuster.

Paul, J. and F. Miller Jr (1990), 'Communitarian and liberal theories of the good', *The Review of Metaphysics*, **43**, 803–30.

Rand, A. (1964), 'The Objectivist Ethics', in *The Virtue of Selfishness*, New York: New American Library, 13–35.

Rasmussen, D.B. (1984), 'Quine and Aristotelian Essentialism', *The New Scholasticism*, **58**, 316–35.

Rasmussen, D.B. (1994), 'The significance for cognitive realism of the thought of John Poinsot', *American Catholic Philosophical Quarterly*, **68**, 409–24.

Rasmussen, D.B. (1995), 'Community versus liberty?', in T.R. Machan and D.B. Rasmussen (eds), *Liberty for the Twenty-First Century*, Lanham, Maryland: Rowman & Littlefield, pp. 259–87.

Rasmussen, D.B. and D.J. Den Uyl (1991), *Liberty and Nature: An Aristotelian Defense of Liberal Order*, La Salle, Illinois: Open Court.

Rawls, J. (1971), *A Theory of Justice*, Cambridge: Harvard University Press.

Rawls, J. (1993), *Political Liberalism*, New York: Columbia University Press.

Raz, J. (1986), *The Morality of Freedom*, Oxford: Clarendon Press.

Raz, J. (1989), 'Facing up: a reply', *University of Southern California Law Review,* **62**, 1153–1235.

Sandell, M. (1982), *Liberalism and the Limits of Justice*, Cambridge: Cambridge University Press.

Selby-Bigge, L.A. (ed.) (1897), *British Moralists*, Oxford: Clarendon Press.

Sowell, T. (1980), *Knowledge and Decisions*, New York: Basic Books.

Strauss, L. (1988), 'Progress or return', in T. Pangle (ed.), *The Rebirth of Classical Political Rationalism*, Chicago: University of Chicago Press, pp. 227–70.

Taylor, C. (1985), 'Atomism', *Philosophy and the Human Sciences: Philosophical Papers*, Vol. 2, Cambridge: Cambridge University Press, pp. 187–210.

Taylor, C. (1989), *Sources of the Self*, Cambridge: Harvard University Press.

Taylor, C. (1991), *The Ethics of Authenticity*, Cambridge: Harvard University Press.

Veatch, H. (1971), *For an Ontology of Morals*, Evanston, Illinois: Northwestern University Press.

Veatch, H. (1985), *Human Rights: Fact or Fancy?*, Baton Rouge and London: Louisiana State University Press.

Veatch, H. (1990), 'Ethical egoism new style: should its trademark be Aristotelian or libertarian?' in *Swimming Against the Current in Contemporary Philosophy*, Washington, DC: The Catholic University of America Press.

Wolfe, C. and J. Hittinger (eds) (1994), *Liberalism at the Crossroads*, Lanham, Maryland: Roman & Littlefield.

Index